The Breaking of Our Healers

The Breaking of Our Healers

·······

*Becoming the Doctor
I Never Planned to Be*

ROBERT ABBOTT, M.D.

TURNING
STONE
PRESS

Copyright © 2022 by Robert Abbott

All rights reserved, including the right to reproduce this work in any form whatsoever, without permission in writing from the publisher, except for brief passages in connection with a review.

Cover design by Jonathan Friedman
Cover concept by Kyle Leahy
Cover art by Getty Images
Print book interior design by Howie Severson

The poem "The Good News" by Thich Nhat Hanh from *Call Me By My True Names* is used with permission of Parallax Press.

Turning Stone Press
San Antonio, TX

Library of Congress Control Number Available on Request.

ISBN 978-1-61852-134-7

10 9 8 7 6 5 4 3 2 1

*To my grandfather and first patient,
Robert L. Stancil*

Contents

PART I
Unraveling into an Awakening   1

PART II
Returning to It All   59

PART III
Wearing a New White Coat   131

PART IV
Love and Letting Go   195

PART V
Where Will You Go to Heal?   249

Epilogue   293
Acknowledgments   295

Part I

Unraveling into an Awakening

⁓ 1 ⁓

The Breaking

Anatomy and the Musculoskeletal System
February 2013

It was a wicked winter night with seven inches of snow, when I began the 1.2-mile walk back from the medical school to my apartment. Raising my hands to my mouth to warm them with my breath, I inhaled the reek of formaldehyde mixed with the essence of wretched nitrile gloves. My knuckles were cracked and bleeding, and my chest burned with every inspiration of cold air. I moved my tongue over my front tooth, devastated by the divot made just days before by an innocuous fork. The cadavers most assuredly had it better than I did.

Paying little attention to the collegiate students around me, I traversed the first of 14th Street's hidden hills.

Wouldn't it be nice to just fall asleep in the snow and never wake up? Peacefully fall away into a deep sleep. No more studying. No more suffering. No one will even notice in the dark; you can just sink softly into the bed of snow.

This turn of thought kept up an insistent message.

Really, it's already 10 o'clock at night on a Wednesday. Just take a little break, rest here in the snow, and you will never have to wake up again.

I wouldn't say for sure what I felt was suicidal, but the thought of disappearing to another world without tests, without snowy hills, without endless suffering was certainly tantalizing.

Two days earlier, while seated in class, I had been hit by a tremendous wave of restlessness and anxiety. While not panicked, I felt millions of tiny electric shocks force my body and mind into a state of disorganized and agitated motion. Afire from this emergent electric storm, I stood up and stumbled out of the auditorium. After a few sips of water, I rushed to the library and tried to resume my studies.
   Like a computer waiting on Apple's "rainbow circle of death," however, I was frozen and incapacitated. My brain yelled out "no more!"
   I had always been a high-functioning student, and to suddenly struggle to read, focus, and integrate new knowledge brought forth only doomsday scenarios. I went home to sleep with the desperate wish that my very being would be reset like my laptop.
   The following morning, though, the "rainbow circle of death" was still cycling.
   Broken souls do not heal with the push of a button.

After another hopeless day of study, I went home and tried to eat my standard dinner, but the food tasted like fermented and rotten vegetables. I threw up a small portion and drank some lemon water to get the taste out of my mouth.

After savoring a second of bitter citrus, I walked into my bathroom to relieve myself and stepped onto the scale to see if I had lost weight because of my recent change in appetite and loose stools.

I was 108 pounds.

I am 5'8".

For most of my life, I had hovered between 120 and 125 pounds, my body shape one of a lean runner and soccer player.

But 108? What in the world was going on?

I was literally wasting away.

Maybe I have cancer. Maybe it's a brain tumor. That's ridiculous. I am 22 years old. But I am 108 pounds, and I can't think anymore! If I don't wither away, I am going to fail out of school and then what will I do? Maybe I have cancer? Maybe it's a brain tumor?

And so it continued.

Back now on the wintry hill, my mind similarly lost in the simple desire for asylum from the previous day's upheaval, I spun faster and faster toward the "comforting" thoughts of relief in snowy sleep and oblivion.

The lights of my apartment complex barely within view, I stumbled through the final yards of my trek. With frozen fingers I unlocked the front door and crashed inside with only enough energy to undress and collapse in bed.

The breaking had begun.

Perhaps God would be kind enough to bring some tea.

2

A Lesson in Mindfulness

UVA Medical School
July 2012

Bright-eyed and bushy-tailed, I awoke on a late July morning in my new apartment, quaintly furnished with my grandparents' antique wooden chests and drawers. With the morning light just beginning to make its way into my eyes, I felt a bead of sweat drip from my brow and realized that, yes, this building constructed in the 1920s and without central AC had not dipped below eighty-three degrees the night before.

Perhaps this cycle of bodily discomfort would only last for the dog days of summer and ease up come October. Until then, I could combat the distress and grime with a routine of bedtime showers, excessive laundry, and accidental prayer. Medical school would involve suffering, glandular secretions and all.

Now any rational person might step back from my situation and identify the weak foundation of the belief *I should accept smelling like Shrek in my own bed because I am in medical school and everything during my training will involve concessions to suffering.* At this point in my life, however, I was unable to utilize basic principles of mindfulness and identify this construction of my consciousness as something without an inherent degree of truth or falsehood. It is a rather simple skill, one that most of us learned in elementary school when we are first challenged to adopt some self-control.

In my own case, that early lesson had centered on a butterfly.

As I sat in my elementary school time-out corner, I steamed with anger after I had disgustingly thrown a box of crayons because my butterfly drawing resembled something more akin to a creature from *Alien* than the cute orange monarch gracing the paper of my "artistic" classmate beside me. All I could think about as I sat in my tiny chair was how poor of an artist I was and how I didn't deserve to use crayons because I would just draw something stupid and not even my mom would like it.

After five minutes of this brooding, my teacher crouched beside me and politely asked, "So do you know why I sent you to the time-out chair?"

I blurted back, "Because I can't draw."

After a small pause, she replied, "No, that's not true. I think you know why I sent you over here, and it does not involve how well you can draw."

Even my young self admitted that I did have a little bit of a self-control problem and she had probably sent me to time-out because of my violent crayon outburst, and not because I couldn't draw a pretty butterfly.

After shedding a few tears, I began to see that I wasn't a "sucky artist" and I could use the crayons if I respected them as property of the whole class.

Little did I know when I was that young that I had just experienced my first lesson in mindfulness.

3

The Fire Hydrant

UVA Medical School Orientation
August 2012

Surrounded by my medical school peers at a round table, I listened to a series of welcoming speeches from the various deans of our prestigious medical school. From dialogues about the positive changes in the curriculum to an orientation about our modern educational facility, everything in our world seemed like it would be a utopian dream. I had even spent the last week engaged in various social orientation activities such as pool parties, peach picking, and a competitive Quidditch match.

Maybe medical school isn't going to be that bad . . .

In an attempt to bring us back to earth a bit, one of the student deans shared a resonating simile for the medical journey that we were about to begin—a variant of a common description given to medical students across the country during their first few days of orientation to impart the amount of work lying ahead.

The material during medical school is like water from a fire hydrant: It will come fast and will never stop even if your mouth is already full.

In medicine, we are often consumed with diagnosing and treating conditions with the view that a pathogen or an insult is the cause of a person's suffering. What is missing from this medical paradigm, however, is the acknowledgment that human suffering can result just as easily from the *absence* of an essential element as it can develop from the presence of something "pathogenic." From this perspective, our deans, even with their deep wells of compassion, could only convey an idea that lacked a basic homeostatic balance, and failed in the moment to encompass a continued exploration of the importance of self-care, the energy required to pursue such a challenging education, and the time I would personally need to spend cultivating my own wellness while I fought the stream from that never-ending fire hydrant.

Do not be blinded by the belief that suffering and disease are only caused by a stressor or an insult. Everything from the absence of certain microbial species in the colon to failing to hear a "good game" following a competitive match of soccer can be as detrimental to our health and well-being as a single cell of Salmonella.

∽ 4 ∽

The Mindful Physician

Medical school is not a cakewalk. Anyone who has completed years of medical training will attest to the tremendous mental and physical rigor required to finish such a daunting endeavor. While I will admit that the fortitude necessary to complete medical education is not exactly the same as the stamina required to complete military training, I see a scary similarity between these environments which both support the development of a stoic demeanor to combat the volatility of the workplace.

Could there be a downside to cultivating stoic soldiers and physicians in such stressful environments?

Exercise physiologists and personal trainers both work with the idea of beneficial stress through the mechanism of *hormesis*. With the correct intervals and intensity of exercise followed by periods of rest and recovery, the body can adapt to the physical stresses and build stronger muscles, increase cellular oxidative capacity, and improve localized blood circulation. In the same way, medical training is designed to put students through various stressors in order to prepare them for the demands of their profession where they will be required to make critical medical decisions no matter the circumstances.

Dr. Hilary Tindle describes an instance in her book *Up* when she was the on-call doctor for an acute care unit. During one of her first nights in the hospital, she was forced to respond to a Code Blue respiratory arrest and began an intubation-cardiac resuscitation protocol to try and revive a dying patient. Relying on the fight-or-flight response from her sympathetic nervous system, she kicked into overdrive to provide immediate lifesaving care. Once the protocol ended, however, she still found herself bathed in the residual symptoms of that adrenaline rush with a racing heartbeat, elevated blood pressure, and sweaty palms. Years later, after a similar Code Blue, Dr. Tindle was astonished to realize that she had no such aftereffects. As a mindful observer of the experience, she no longer allowed herself to be caught inside the reactive "autonomic whirlwind" and responded instead with a resilient spirit that enabled her to return to a state of relative calm following the administration of lifesaving care. At the foundation of her stress response was a mental stability and understanding that *I am a capable physician* and *I am emotionally and mentally prepared to attend to this patient's needs without being consumed by the internal stress systems of my body.*

We desperately need our physicians to display the type of stability and resilience portrayed by Dr. Tindle; however, our current medical education system does not cultivate the compassionate, mindful, and resilient healer, but rather the disillusioned, detached, and emotionally distant healer burdened by a system crushing her from the inside out.

To enact this change within medical education and health care as a whole would require reforming a culture that goes beyond any single person or institution. But that doesn't mean that every individual is powerless to alter their personal trajectory. Transforming oneself from a distant, white coat–armored medical practitioner to a compassionate, reflective, and mindful physician takes an individual commitment that no hospital or academic system can impose. I wish resiliency training alone were the answer, but resiliency training while you are still wading in a swamp simply improves your ability to survive long enough to acknowledge that you are soaking wet.

5

My Brother, Agitation

Biochemistry, Genetics, and Immunology
October 2012

After two months at UVA, I felt confident and knowledgeable as a young medical student. As we studied biochemical pathways alongside genetics and immunology, I incorporated much of my previous undergraduate chemistry and biology work into its applications in medicine. For many of my colleagues with limited scientific backgrounds, however, the transition was much more demanding, and the stress began to accumulate.

As part of my academic endeavors, I studied regularly with one of my closest new friends, Dilawar Khokhar. Together, we spent hours talking about various topics from the methylation cycle and homozygosity to viral replication and the antibiotics used to treat the stubborn bacteria *Pseudomonas aeruginosa*. Our verbal discussions and his feedback not only prepared me for our numerous medical assessments, but made meaning out of our endless daily grind. Even when we toiled away in silence, I found comfort with my dear friend, another human being dealing with the torrent from the very same fire hydrant.

With the adoption of "The Next Generation Curriculum" just two years before, the UVA School of Medicine provided all of its resources via electronic texts, journals, handouts, and reading packets. The exhaustive educational material was like an electronic version of the Library of Congress.

Where in the hell did one begin?

With my perfectionist tendencies on blatant display, I downloaded all of the educational resources using my Evernote note-taking program and created, in essence, my own "library" for school. For this end alone, I spent at least two hours a week, seated and staring at an excessively illuminated laptop screen, with my fingers involved in a ridiculous choreography of clicking, typing, and keyboard manipulation just to organize the materials into separate notebooks. At times I was so drained by this organizational task that when it came to actually *looking* at the educational material, my attention was about as good as a seven-year-old in a moon bounce playground. The hours of sitting and staring at screens felt like purgatory and only exacerbated my internal fire of unrelenting agitation. As if my cells themselves were constantly being singed by an unknowable flame, I sought constant forms of stimulation to somehow release the growing restlessness.

In an attempt to combat both the unrelenting agitation and my cognitive disdain for my sedentary oblivion, I inserted physical movement of all kinds into every open second of my day. While my breaks for movement away from a computer screen seemed like the perfect antidote to the long slogs through an endless ocean of reading material, my restlessness continued unabated and my demand for distracting movement became insatiable.

Day after day I went through the unsustainable routine of study and activity, study and activity. Sometimes I stole away to the sanctuary of my bicycle, riding for hours as far away as I could get from school, only to return home for another meal and another reading assignment. Sometimes I would wake at 5 a.m. to walk to the school pool to swim in relative seclusion before walking still more for a morning full of lectures. Throw in some afternoon weight lifting sessions and late-night wanders around deserted halls of the medical school and you have yourself a day packed with productivity without the slightest sprinkle of recovery, rest, or calm.

I needed someone to take out my batteries.

I needed to know there was another way.

⁓ 6 ⁑

Touching God

Anatomy and the Musculoskeletal System
February 2013

In college, I participated in a men's Bible study with a group of supportive human beings. I felt safe, alive, and free as I studied scriptures and shared space with a gathering of vulnerable men. I grew my faith leaps and bounds and found meaning in this collective. After I started medical school, however, science took precedence over faith, and God had no real estate in my consciousness.

By the time the shrill February air was scratching my sunken cheeks, I was not practicing any religion. I was not searching for or believing in miracles.

I was simply searching for the sirens on my godforsaken hills.

After my escape from the wintry mix, I quickly collapsed in bed and fell into a dream.

From within this dream, I stared at a body sleeping away on a bed eerily similar to mine, in a room eerily similar to my own. In a moment of unspeakable incredulity, I suddenly realized that the young man swallowed up by a mammoth of a bed was not a stranger.

The young man was me.

As I looked around the space, I noticed that the room was not just similar to my own, the room *was* my own. Every last detail, precise and perfect.

Dumbfounded, it came to me that my experience was not a dream as I understood them. As I moved now to interact with what I perceived as my emaciated body, everything became brilliantly white.

Utter silence. Utter light.

Despite the immensity of this shift, I was surprisingly not afraid.

I felt for the first time the surrender of complete calm.

It was as if I had finally fallen asleep in the snow.

As I basked in this calming light, I suddenly became aware of what I can only describe as another's thoughts.

There was no speech, no noise. It was as if someone were speaking directly into my own consciousness.

"I will give you your life back, but you must commit it to relieving the suffering of others."

"Isn't that precisely what I am trying to do?" I tried to scream out.

"When you wake up, you will know what to do."

The next moment, I was awake.

And without any rational reason, I knew precisely what to do.

7

The Heart Awakens

UVA Medical Center
February 2013

It was 4:30 in the morning, but I couldn't go back to sleep. My mind raced with the pressing thought that I must stop and get help.

The batteries had come out.

There had to be another way.

Some people talk about the "fear of God," and while images of fire and brimstone pervade much of our culture in connection with these words, what I had just felt was anything but destructive. Having just experienced what might be best described as serene urgency, I now had a degree of clarity about my purpose and the positive compulsion to manifest what God had seemingly commanded moments earlier. While still struggling with the details of how to even begin a manifestation of His commandments, I made my way later that morning to my dean's office.

"I need help. I can't live like this anymore."

She saw my suffering and recognized the pain in my voice. She shared that it was common for students to take time away from medical school for many reasons and I would have up to six years to complete the four years of schooling. Relieved to hear that I could still finish on a modified timeline, I listened as she went on to describe that I could take a year off to seek restored health and resume at the same point the next year with the next class.

After a practical discussion about my medical leave, she sent me over to Student Health to see one of the primary care clinicians. In what seemed like only seconds, the clinician was looking me over with a fair degree of disbelief. Without words, she conveyed a sense of extreme concern—as if she expected me to die at any moment. Given my low weight and mental health issues, she recommended inpatient hospitalization at the University of North Carolina–Chapel Hill Neurosciences Hospital on their Eating Disorders Unit. As I tried to make sense of her recommendations, my mind leapt to the idea of being in a hospital.

How in the world would I fit in? I don't have an eating disorder. Is she recommending this because I am underweight? Won't this place be full of young women with whom I have nothing in common? How is this a part of actually getting better?

As I returned from this worrisome reverie, she continued to express her concern over my current state of health. In addition to her recommendation of an inpatient hospitalization, she insisted I be admitted overnight to the cardiac observation unit at the UVA Medical Center.

What in the world was that for?

On the third floor of the medical center, I was strapped with monitors to assess my heart rate throughout the evening. Before I had time to get disillusioned with my first experience as a hospitalized patient, several of my close friends came to visit me on the other side of the gown. Bathed in one of the most touching acts of humanity I had ever experienced, I struggled to find the emotional language and expressiveness to tell them how much it meant to know that I was seen, that I was cared for, that I was loved.

After my friends departed our moment of human connection in that sterile hospital room, I was left for the night with my dad and a symphony of beeps and alarms. While I had been in a fairly lucid and functional state for most of the day, I now slipped back into the cycling of the "rainbow circle of death," exhausted from the energy expenditure required to get me from my bed and the out-of-body experience to the hospital and the steps beyond. Back in the world of chaos and confusion, I fell into a restless sleep, waking several times throughout the night with the thought that my arm was broken, that I had just had major abdominal surgery, or that my heart had stopped altogether.

The following morning, after I shared an egg omelet with my father, the medical team notified me that I would be discharged for the moment with a plan for admission to UNC in the weeks to come. While the laboratory findings from my stay were essentially unremarkable, the medical team noted that the telemetry monitors tracking my heart rate had shown a slow rate at multiple times throughout the night of around thirty-five beats per minute. While athletes commonly have heart rates in the forties, heart rates in the thirties border on an incompatibility with life. As my body struggled to muster enough energy to power my heart muscle, my metabolic systems were slowing my heart rate to the brink.

My heart was screaming out to be healed.

8

What Healing Is

UNC Hospital
February 2013

At the entrance of the Eating Disorders Unit at the UNC Neurosciences Hospital, I was asked to relinquish my personal belongings as well as any items such as belts, strings from sweatpants, and even headphones with leads that could be used for self-harm. I understood the rationale for such policies—*but how can a person heal in a place with such rules?* While my passive thoughts of slipping away into the snow and leaving this world behind had long since receded, my heart wrestled with the idea of how healing could occur amidst the assumption that patients were a risk to their own existence. Intertwined with this thought, however, rested my own dissolving denial of the truth that I had walked myself to the brink of self-destruction.

I *had* been a risk to my own flourishing.

A risk I no longer wished to be.

At my first group session in yet another remarkably sterile hospital room, I met the other patients on the Eating Disorders Unit, and my previous suspicions about the gender diversity of the unit were confirmed.

I was the only man.

With women ranging in age from early adolescence into their late sixties, my shredded masculinity and shrouded femininity together wondered from what dark abyss had these souls emerged.

From what hell and suffering did they seek to escape?
Into what love did we all need to surrender?

After my introductory group session, we moved to one of the main meals of the day. With seemingly half of the daily schedule made up of group meals and snacks, my mind raced thinking of the relative torture this must be to many of the patients who perceived food not as the sustenance of life, but its destroyer. As I sat at the table with the other patients, I felt years of punishment, restriction, purging, disgust, and fear—fear of annihilation, fear of inadequacy, fear of fatness, fear of uncertainty, fear of being loved.

One of the women was so malnourished she required feeding through a nasogastric tube. Visible externally, the tube coursed into a nostril and snaked its way down her esophagus where it unceremoniously deposited tasteless nutrition into her stomach to support her depleted physical form. Another of the girls looked no older than ten, yet here we were, breathing the same air with the same name tag that marked us as "suffering patient."

While every patient on the unit presented some disordered relationship with food, merely categorizing us as patients with eating disorders missed the real problems, the real suffering, the real humanity that had yet to find love in the world. Conventional medicine can describe phenomena such as symptoms and behavior rather precisely, but what conventional medicine lacks more than anything is the ability to describe the human experience, to unwrap the soul from the diagnosis so that both the physician and the patient can finally see the why underneath the tip of the phenomenological iceberg—an unraveling existence wanting to feel whole again, a desperate mind knowing this can't be all there is.

As I looked into the faces of equally lost souls, searching themselves for the light tucked away by God, I was overcome by the truth that these women—no matter how biologically distinct—could be nothing other than "me." We could only ever be mirrors to the parts of ourselves we had fought to destroy, to accept, to love. Housed in other human forms lay the femininity in me I had never bothered to nourish, to hold, to let be. Hidden behind their ovaries and uteri lay the masculinity in me that had fallen from society's ladder of achievement. In others there could only be love. In others there could only ever be the oneness of us all.

Over the first two weeks of my hospital stay, I found my legs disfigured by unrecognizable swelling, my abdomen in a perpetual state of bloated unease from the caloric excess, and my thighs greasy from a testosterone replacement gel that offered the promise of artificial masculinity. I came to know the intricacies of my excretory schedule as I voided into plastic urinals with patient assistants tracking my collective output. I awoke from nightmares only to turn on fluorescent lights that illuminated my emaciated body.

I eventually wrote a letter to my "past self" to forgive him for ever leading me here. I forgave him for his unsustainable solutions for the unrelenting agitation. I forgave him for his excessive bike rides, his perfectionism, and his disastrous rigidity. I forgave him for his desire to academically excel at the expense of true nourishment. I forgave him for forgoing the observance of his physical form in favor of books and screens that promised him accolades and a future seemingly worth living.

In the end, all I could do was forgive and love him, for it was precisely his courageous leap of faith that would allow me to feel for the first time what healing really is.

9

A Human Being, Not a Human Doing

UNC Hospital
February 2013

During my third week on the Eating Disorders Unit at the UNC Neurosciences Hospital, I was moved to the combined inpatient and outpatient program and tasted my first bit of freedom. I had made significant strides to combat my agitation, restlessness, and mental anxiety, and my overall health had improved. But I was by no means ready to walk on my own two feet, as the seeds of my mental, spiritual, and emotional awakening were just being planted. The afternoon schedule was full of group activities, including both a cognitive behavioral therapy (CBT) session where I learned to evaluate my thoughts and feelings and how they influenced my actions and behaviors, and an acceptance and commitment therapy (ACT) session where I learned to mindfully recognize my thoughts and opinions and accept that my being was something separate from all the craziness running through my head.

While I enjoyed these groups, my heart longed to participate in a new activity called "Mindful Stretching." The name seemed rather strange, but the implication of some form of exercise was quite enticing. I was all too eager to see how well I could extend my hamstrings and much less concerned with the requirements of doing it "mindfully." When I asked the other patients about Mindful Stretching, I encountered rather indifferent attitudes and sometimes downright disgust for this weekly group activity. I had entered the program at UNC with a perspective open to any potential therapies that would bring my mind and body a respite from the hours of medical school suffering, so I was not about to discount what might possibly be in store based on the impressions of my fellow patients.

As we unfolded our yoga mats—although the term *yoga* was never used—and collected various props—which appeared to be just a hodgepodge of cushions, blocks, and for some reason straps—I came to peace within the dimly lit room. The walls, while still clinically white, emanated a novel softness finally free of the torrid fluorescent drone. Spaced mere inches apart from the other attendees, I lay in an unexpected surrender. In a soothing voice, the lead caregiver invited a gentle peace to all those in the room who desired its beckoning serenity. With each curious, instructed movement I awakened to the persistence of my beating heart and the rhythmic joy that was our collective vital symphony.

While I had previously participated in exercises involving biofeedback, diaphragmatic breathing, and progressive muscle relaxation during the first two weeks of my inpatient stay, Mindful Stretching opened the doors to a sanctuary where gears did not grind and minds did not run on hamster wheels. The disordered rationalizations I had constructed to appease my agitation and compulsivity were vanquished by the simplicity and stillness of this sanctuary.

Had I really possessed the keys to this place all along?

Through a gentle sequence of asana including Cakravakasana/Cat-Cow, Vajrasana/Kneeling, Bhujangasana/Cobra, and Tadasana/Mountain, I genuinely felt connected to my body's physiology. With the application of a conscious awareness to my body, I had the power to not only manipulate its physiological processes, such as heart rate, respiratory rate, and thermal regulation, but I could attune to the sensations and feedback from my cells trying "to speak" about their current state of health and being. Since I had lived the majority of my life completely disconnected from my body's physiological language, I could only describe the crude sensations of relative pain and temperature. To associate a fast heart rate with anxiety, shallow respirations with poor posture and disturbed breathing mechanics, and tremulous and fatigued muscles with the need for rest or relaxation was remarkably challenging. I was essentially deaf to anything my body had attempted to convey through such channels. To avoid being suddenly overwhelmed with this newfound physiologic awareness, I directed my attention solely to my breathing and the guidance for intentionally directed physical movements. Through Mindful Stretching and all of its innocuous glory, I found an outlet to restoratively move my body, calm my physical agitation, and breathe with the awareness that I did not need to go anywhere or really do anything to experience inner peace.

As the session ended, I was overcome once again by my racing mind.

When is the next session? How can I get a yoga mat? Is there an iPad app I can download to practice some sequences? Should I read a book?

Amazingly, rather than return to the chaotic world of my usual racing mental state, I realized that my new interest in adopting a personal yoga practice did not need to be a rapid pursuit, but could rather be a gradual incorporation of a new way of being. I could finally see that I was never meant to be a human *doing*, but a human *being*.

~ 10 ~

The Purple Icon

UNC Hospital
March 2013

Still buzzing from the birth of my new yoga practice, I attempted to find some answers for "The Voice" from my out-of-body experience.

Surely this path of yoga, of growing self-awareness, of deepening spiritual practice would lead to a lessening of suffering. But what practically was I supposed to do?

While I held on to a conditional spot in my medical school, contingent on my medical recovery during my yearlong leave, I was not entirely certain I wanted to go back to school.

Who in their right mind would want to go back into that fire?

While medical school was the setting of my ultimate unraveling, I had walked a road of unsustainable achievement for years. I was class president throughout most of high school, where I excelled academically and played team sports nearly every season. I graduated summa cum laude from the College of William and Mary while I worked as an emergency room scribe for over two years. I had even excelled during my first few months of medical school up until the breaking. If medical school was still on the "road of achievement," I could not imagine I would ever go back.

With my transition to the partial hospitalization program, I was granted a few more privileges, the most important being the opportunity to have a now approved gift—an iPod Nano. While I was well aware that this small handheld device would open a world of music and idyllic harmony, I had somehow managed to make it to 2013 without listening to a single podcast. I hadn't even *heard of* a podcast until I saw the purple icon on my screen.

After I clicked my way down into the purple abyss, I discovered an overwhelming array of podcast conversations. From multipart series and self-help podcasts to conversations about health and spirituality, I unearthed an auditory treasure trove. Naturally gravitating to the health and wellness podcasts, I stumbled upon one called "The Healthy Skeptic." Started by acupuncturist and functional medicine researcher Chris Kresser, the podcast was a scientific exploration into nutrition and integrative medicine as well as what he called "an evolutionary or ancestral perspective on health." While I had some interest in nutrition—harnessing a misguided awareness about the nourishing foods I should consume from popular media suggestions—I was not a natural medicine connoisseur and hadn't grown up with general experience of the dietary and lifestyle habits to optimally support wellness. Although I had eaten an above average amount of vegetables as a child, my family still consumed the typical "standard American diet" and followed no particular pattern of holistic medical guidance. I had not come to iTunes to learn about nutrition, herbs, or mindfulness practices. Yet, despite all of the baggage of my history and family circumstances, I listened to a conversation Chris was having about polyunsaturated fats.

As he delved into the differences between omega-3 and omega-6 fats and how our food supply had become a tsunami of heavily processed omega-6 oils, I was left speechless. I thought about my diet—the "standard American diet"—and the implications for our society as a whole. Captivated by the scientific core of his discussions as well as the humility of his curious inquiry, I could not get enough of Chris's conversations. Over mere weeks, I listened to more and more podcasts. From conversations with Stephan Guyenet, Ph.D., about food reward and hyperpalatability to engaging discussions with Chris Masterjohn, Ph.D., about lipid metabolism and cholesterol, I entered a whole new world that had blossomed into existence with the simple click of a purple podcast icon.

With my mind freed from the hours of medical school reading, I stumbled upon a radical idea.

Why not make my own "medical school" from these podcasts?

Using just a simple spiral notebook and my iPod Nano, my mind went to work as my hands produced pages and pages of podcast notes within days. As I found more podcasts and websites through the guests on Chris's show, I unleashed an exploding world of information and unfathomable possibility. In a matter of weeks, my entire foundation of self-care and wellness had been shaken to its core. With the integration of my newly developed mindfulness practice and yoga routine and my growing understanding of ancestral, whole foods nutrition, the days of listlessness and the "rainbow circle of death" faded further and further away.

While the picture I paint here is one of beautiful enlightenment, the truth of the experience was much more brutal.

What in the hell had I been doing for all my life? Why hadn't I been practicing yoga since childhood? Why did our society support the consumption of a nutrient-poor, pro-inflammatory diet, and what in the world were we learning in medical school?

With the early realization that cynicism, pity, and anger would not lead me to compassion and an end of suffering, I quickly left such narratives behind and returned to the beauty that was my second chance at life.

I was not a student here to achieve high grades and pass tests. I was here to learn how human suffering developed and how I could, with all means possible, lessen its presence in our complex world.

≈ 11 ≈

Researching Love

Charlottesville
April 2013

During the final weeks of my time at UNC, I evaluated what exactly I wanted to pursue as part of my medical school leave. While my greatest commitment would remain the continued improvement of my physical and mental health, I did not know how to practically construct a productive and meaningful life. With the birth of my "personal podcast medical school" that focused on the areas of spirituality as well as integrative and ancestral medicine, I understood that my evolving approach to healing would be radically different from the education I had started to pursue in the fall of 2012. Burdened with worries over a return to medical school that did not align with my developing interests and desires for self-care, I redirected my energies into other pursuits until the decision on whether or not to return to medical school became clear.

While looking into flexible job opportunities that aligned with my healing endeavors, I found a research project through the School of Medicine conducted by a general surgery resident who wanted to explore the role of positive psychology in the care of cardiac surgery patients. Intrigued and at the same time confused about a general surgeon's interest in positive psychology, I sent a message to the resident to express my unique situation and desire to help. After he sent a rapid reply, the surgeon and I arranged a meeting in the hospital cafeteria—the same one where I had eaten the omelet during my overnight hospital stay in February. As part of a research year for his general surgery residency, he had designed a multidimensional study to see how a reflective interview followed by gratitude journaling could improve outcomes in patients undergoing major heart surgery. Since he needed a research assistant to get the study off the ground, he was eager to bring me on board to launch the project.

After a few short weeks of organization, the study got underway, and I found myself inside the cardiac surgery clinic ready to enroll potential study participants. Given the nature of our study, we sought individuals who would undergo major cardiac procedures—either open-heart surgery to replace certain valves or surgery to bypass diseased blood vessels supplying the heart itself with oxygen. The risk of death during or shortly after these procedures varies depending on the health of the patient, but in general they carry a nontrivial risk of dying.

In my role as clinical researcher, my time with these suffering humans lay at the proverbial last stop, hours into their journey of testing, waiting, and meeting with the surgeon. As my first day crawled to a close, I ushered my only potential study participant, a visibly tired, but curious older man, into my makeshift office. We sat together at a small round table, and I shared the details of the study. Enlivened by my youth and our intentions to utilize nonpharmacological therapies, the man perked up from his medical routine passivity as if I myself had surgically repaired his heart with the mere softness of my eyes. After a few clicks on my screen, I determined via our randomization scheme that he would participate in our "study intervention," which involved an introductory interview designed to elicit positive reflection and feelings of gratefulness. Within the confines of a closet of an office, a young man easily mistaken for a college freshman and an aged gentleman nearly three times his years stepped into their first "experiment."

"For what are you most grateful?"
"From what or whom do you receive support, care, and love?"

As we walked further into the story of the man before me, I sat back and listened to his tales of faith, suffering, and supportive wonder. He told me about his inability to walk uphill to his mailbox and his challenges to simply hold his grandkids. He shared the deep importance of his church and how his small community was already planning to pay for extra medical expenses and provide him with food during the arduous recovery period. He poured out the years of love showered on him by a partner who continued to work in order to provide financial support for their larger family.

And so we continued.

"How do you feel the surgery will impact your life?"
"What is something you are looking forward to doing after the surgery?"

Moved nearly to tears, I was left wordless more than once by what this virtual stranger shared with me. While

I knew the most important aspects of his medical history and was quite fluent with medical jargon from my years as a scribe, I sat now in the halls of prestigious cardiac clinic uncovering a humanity that was everything but "medical."

"How did you come to take part in this research study?" the man asked me after responding to my final question.

Unsure how to reply to his table-turning inquiry, I halted my scribbles and pondered his invited reflection. After perhaps ten seconds of pure silence, I responded.

"I was sick and finally decided I wanted to be well."

Over the next few months, I continued to have more of these encounters where I was graced to hear the life stories and deepest longings of nearly twenty-five study participants. From grandmothers in their eighties who wanted to walk at their grandkid's weddings to men in their forties who had already lived through multiple surgeries to repair dysfunctional valves present at birth, I took in the hopes and dreams of a group of humans who all simply wanted to be well.

While all these patients stitched themselves into the mosaic of my own healing trajectory, one man managed without conscious intent to lovingly drill straight into my slowly healing heart. Living just over the border in West Virginia, the man I will call "Jeremiah" was a veritable health disaster with an accent I struggled mightily to ever comprehend. With organs failing left and right, Jeremiah had been to the brink of death and back more times than I had fingers. How could I offer him the support he and so many desperately needed?

One evening, I sat down for a final phone call to Jeremiah in order to complete his last follow-up interview. I had been greeted only by busy signals for the last four weeks as I attempted to make this final call and had not seen or spoken to Jeremiah since he had left the hospital after surgery over three months earlier.

This time, though, I was pleasantly surprised to hear a ringtone. After five full rings, however, my early optimism was replaced by accumulated grief. I was moving to place the handset back on the receiver just as an almost inaudible utterance came through.

"Hellar, this Jermi'."

"Hello, Jeremiah, this is Rob Abbott from the positive psychology research study. I'm calling to check in with you to see how things are going and if you would be willing to answer a few questions?"

"Surely be, it's good to hear from you, son. I hate to admit it, but I lost that dern journal thing you gave me. It ain't bother me that much though as I can't write that good anyway. But ye be proud 'cause I've been thinkin' them positive thoughts each day. The Good Lord bless me like sumthin' else. I miss you, son, whyn't you call me sooner?"

Without words to explain my previous attempts nor the ability to comprehend my own overflowing emotions, I moved us through his final survey questions and the dance of this unforeseen but surprisingly intimate relationship.

After I wrapped up my final question, Jeremiah jumped back into our curious dialogue.

"When you callin' next, son? Yur welcome over this way whenever. You got my address in that computer machine of yurs, I reckon."

Researching Love

"It's been really wonderful to talk with you, Jeremiah, but this was actually the last phone call we have for the study. You are all finished now!"

"Finished? Well dern. So you ain't calling again? You've been good to me, son. God's got a good ole' plan for you. Damn good plan."

Medicine, as I knew it, would never just be medicine again.

12

A Friend Where You Least Expect It

Positive Psychology Research—UVA Medical Center
May 2013

While I made friends in the positive psychology research world, my world outside of the cardiac clinic was slow to grow. During my hospitalization I recognized that much of my suffering had come from isolation. Even though it was isolation I had created myself because of my rigidity and excessive studying, the seclusion had eaten away at my well-being, and my heart could not tolerate being alone.

As part of my work with the positive psychology research study, I took regular walking breaks out of the clinic through the hospital lobby to get some sun and fresh air. With the establishment of my "regular route," I saw some of the same people occupying their posts in the hospital lobby. Workers on the patient experience team, these individuals escorted patients and families from the hospital entrance to the main lobby and directed discharged patients to their cars for their journeys home.

One day during one of my usual walking breaks, I was greeted by a joyful, middle-aged black man named George and these unexpected words, "You always seem so happy, with that smile on your face walking around here. I couldn't help but say something after seeing you so many times."

His words were the most sincere and unexpected invitation to friendship I had ever received. I was overwhelmed with the feeling that I was being noticed for who I was and not for what I did. From this simple interaction was born an evolving friendship that led to regular conversations about our own pasts and how we had come to this place.

I learned that George had left a stressful job in HR and made a life pivot to the patient experience team in order to better support his ailing heart. Interwoven with his stories and laughter, I shared for the first time the unexplainable days of my early recovery and how I had stepped away from a stressful world myself in order to heal years of perfectionist rigidity and physical deterioration.

"We got the same heart, Rob. You can see it a mile away. We just gotta fill them up as much as we empty them out."

While you can already likely sense the deep meaning this new human connection had for me, the true profundity of this interaction taking place in the hospital setting needs a lengthier explanation.

From dismissive eyes to hurried gaits, the hospital is not a place of regular human connection. You will often find yourself without a response to eye contact or even a hello on more occasions than not. It is as if the job of caring for others, for fulfilling our roles as medical technicians supplants all other jobs and needs including that of connecting with the strangers we encounter and even those we call colleagues and friends. The hospital catacombs are a bizarre place, one where you feel that even a simple hello, nod, or smile will derail the efforts of medical technicians needing every ounce of energy and acumen to complete their twelve-, sixteen- or twenty-four-hour shifts.

I am not surprised, however, by the distant manner of most healthcare workers. By the time most nurses, surgeons, or internists finish their education, they are burned out and at least partially, if not totally, numb to the lack of humanity in much of the traditional hospital system. To take it a step further, I would suggest that there is even an unconscious motivation in many to avoid human interactions, as it is too much to bear that much of their job is devoid of the real compassion and healing they might have envisioned as part of a career in health care.

So you see, making friends—really deep and loving friendships—from seemingly the most minute of encounters in the hospital defies rational explanation. Rationality, however, would not stop these two humans from embracing their true nature in an act of loving rebellion to an institution and culture that had mightily lost their way.

13

The Nurses

UVA School of Nursing
June 2013

In the summer of 2012 during my preparations for med school, I had serendipitously connected with two incoming classmates, Thomas Ball and Nick Hac. Brought together through Thomas's query on our school's housing forum, we bonded quickly as we searched together for suitable housing to begin our graduate education. Settling for "old but stylish," we passed on AC in favor of a tiny kitchen and a porch to endure the heat.

I mean how much time were we going to spend in this place anyway?

Somewhere in our first few conversations, Thomas and I had discovered just how small our worlds were. Separated by nearly seven years in age, we had actually graduated from the same independent middle and high school and had even both attended the College of William and Mary, with his family still living in Williamsburg and mine in nearby Yorktown. Crawling back into the bowels of middle school, I could even remember Thomas as a then senior, more akin to Iron Man than a disastrous teenager trying to figure out this impossible world.

Through our early months in school together as the "three medical school amigos," Thomas, Nick, and I found time to enjoy each other's company despite the growing flow of the medical school fire hydrant. By early fall 2012, however, my rigidity and our accumulated stress had erased our already evaporating time to be human. Despite sharing the same space, I was cut off from the pulse of our accidental family and the beating truth that none of us is ever alone.

After my return from the hospital to our shared apartment in April 2013, I sought to reconnect with Thomas and Nick. Seeing the torrent of the medical school fire hydrant still coursing steadily through their lives, I often felt despondent about what I had seemingly given up.

Would I ever make it back to prove to them and the world that I could handle the fire hydrant?

Once while Thomas and I shared an evening cup of tea, he asked me if I had been to a meditation or yoga class at the nursing school.

"There are meditation classes at the School of Nursing?!" I asked in astonishment.

"Yeah, there are several free classes every week in McLeod Hall. We can go together sometime if you like."

"That would be awesome! Where's McLeod Hall? The main campus?" I asked.

"Right next to the med school . . ." he deadpanned.

You might assume that as a student, I would have been intimately aware of all the academic buildings in the vicinity of my regular habitation, but that was far from the truth. During my early, narrowed days of study, I had no idea that just yards from the main medical school building existed rooms dedicated by the School of Nursing for reflective practice and self-care.

While I could explain my lack of knowledge about the School Nursing as a result of my previous, extreme rigidity, I recognized that my limited awareness about their academic system was simply the tip of a worrisome iceberg. While you might reasonably think that health science students like medical students and nursing students have significant overlap and professional interactions during their years of education with the goal of maximal preparation to work together in environments that require collaboration and compassionate understanding, you would sadly be quite wrong.

For the nonmedical folks reading this, this may come as a complete shock, but I'm sure the medical practitioners among us are likely nodding in agreement and acknowledging the paucity of meaningful professional interactions between students of the various healthcare professions. While we face many issues within medical education, the lack of meaningful professional engagement between health science students is one of the biggest and least discussed, and it is greatly affecting our ability to provide personalized, compassionate care to patients.

Just a few years earlier, the School of Nursing (SON), led by their then Dean Dorrie Fontaine and Susan Bauer-Wu, had started a schoolwide Compassionate Care Initiative (CCI). The purpose of the CCI was to provide a space for their students to grow and maintain their own health while they built the resilience needed to deliver compassionate care to the patients they encountered during their training and beyond. As part of the initiative, the SON devised a weekly schedule of meditation, yoga, and other gatherings that were free for students and even open to the wider public. While I was not an active UVA student at the time, I could still attend free meditations and yoga as Thomas had suggested and meet other like-minded students in the health sciences.

Was this what God meant by miracles?

Days after Thomas's revelatory news, I attended a yoga class led by nurse and yoga teacher Esther Lozano. After forgiving myself for not realizing what had been mere yards from my school, I picked out one of the yoga mats provided and set it on the floor in a room filled with about ten people. With her gentle, yet determined voice, Esther invited the collective to begin our group practice. As she guided us through various sequences, I was immediately taken back to the space of serene wonder first experienced at UNC during my sessions of "Mindful Stretching." While I had continued a personal yoga practice that included about twenty minutes of asana in the morning and at least ten minutes of intentional meditation in the evening, this was the first communal gathering I had experienced since UNC. After the sixty-minute class was over, I shared my deep gratitude with Esther for the generosity of her heart.

"I am just getting into a yoga practice and can't believe you guys offer this at the nursing school. This is such a gift. Thank you!"

"It was lovely to meet you, Rob, and I appreciate you coming," she reciprocated with a joyful smile. "Maybe I'll see you next week?"

"Of course."

As I started my walk back to my apartment, my mind raced with grateful wonder.

What were the chances that I would find a home and family just yards from my medical school to develop my evolving perspective of the healer and healing?

In this precise moment—despite my questions and doubts about conventional medical school education, despite my concerns that I would never be able to practice medicine in the ways I was beginning to envision, and despite my fear that medical school would steal back my time for self-care and true nourishment—I finally knew that I belonged in Charlottesville and that I would return to school and grow something I couldn't yet fully imagine.

∽ 14 ∾

A New Plan

UVA School of Medicine
December 2013

Nearly a year after I began my medical leave, the papers were finalized. I was rejoining the medical school class of 2017. Since November, I had rigorously planned my reintroduction into academic life. I was determined to do medical school differently.

To start, I openly acknowledged that I could not study everything assigned. I could not get remotely close. While as an undergrad I had devoted as much time as was necessary to master the assigned material, medical school did not play by the same rules. While the medical school curriculum provided guidelines or learning objectives for how to best direct my study, I could not read everything available. I would not have a complex working knowledge of every topic presented. I would not study everything.

With my acceptance of the tasks that would be impossible to complete, I also realized that with the medical school's pass-fail system, all I needed to do was to meet the passing mark necessary for progression. For a recovering perfectionist, this was quite freeing. While I did not plan to just skirt by, I acknowledged that I was not in medical school for grades because they essentially did not exist.

In addition to accepting the pass-fail system and accepting that I could not and would not study everything assigned, I recognized that I also needed a new approach to the self-directed curriculum. With only a handful of mandatory lectures to attend each week, our school provided me with a great ability to learn and master the material in whatever ways I chose.

Through my discovery of podcasts and the realm of auditory learning, I had hours of prerecorded and recorded medical school lectures beckoning as my destined form of pedagogical exploration. With the provided recordings, I could listen to the medical school curriculum on my own terms and at my own speed. Adding in gentle movement along the roads and trails of Charlottesville, I could find, dare I say, pure joy in medical education.

As part of my increasing preparations for the return to the fire hydrant, I stared directly at the device that had been so destructive during my early medical school studies: my laptop. While all of my curricular materials would be accessed online, *did I really need to spend every waking moment glued to a screen?*

During my awakening to podcasts, I started to handwrite notes in spiral notebooks. After the initial transcription, I went back through my notes and highlighted sections according to a specified schema in order to solidify my understanding of the topics discussed. Amazingly, by slowing down to write and highlight various sections, I brought greater efficiency to my studies.

I was about to become the guy with the highlighters.

Although I had checked off many of the most important boxes for my evolving study habits and perspective, I still needed to figure out another problem: the sitting. The sitting in lectures and the library had been so destructive during my first phase of school, so I could not rely on standard library tables and desks to survive. With the help of my father, I purchased a standing desk that I could adjust based on whether I wanted to sit or stand. While this may sound like a minor detail, many of my friends and colleagues that have seen my desk (it is still in my clinic office to this day) have heard me say that it was likely the most important item I owned during medical school.

As I stood at my newly constructed standing desk, all the details of my plan to engage with medical school now in place, I stared across the room at The Elephant—the central question I had yet to face.

In between bites of fluffernutter, that Elephant calmly asked,

"What exactly are you going back to study?"

In the span of ten months, I had acquired an education in nutrition and clinical biochemistry that would surpass nearly 99 percent of my peers and professors. I had attended a conference entitled the Symposium of Yoga Research and had continued to develop my own yoga practice. I had read numerous books and studies about the role of nutrition, lifestyle, and mindfulness in positively impacting disease. While I couldn't definitively say that I wouldn't be exposed to such topics in school, I knew that the hours devoted to nutritional and integrative medicine could be counted on my own two hands.

What exactly was I here to study?

Given the marginalization of integrative and alternative practitioners in most traditional medicine circles, I realized that in order for supervising doctors to take me seriously, I would have to operate at a tier above my medical school peers when it came to foundational clinical knowledge. A supervising doctor can laugh off a student who doesn't understand the pharmacokinetics and mechanism of action of certain medications like metoprolol, but can they ignore a student who demonstrates how certain medications will deplete nutrients and cites research supporting the synergistic utilization of a medicine and nutritional supplement combination? I only knew a few rules of the medical game, but I was here to relieve suffering and to have my progress impeded because of ignorance was not an option.

In an attempt to reconcile the potential conflict between the time needed to study the mechanisms of action of various drugs with my desire to never prescribe certain drugs at any point in my clinical career, I came back again and again to the mantra: *relieve suffering and do no harm with all the tools available*. With my developing understanding of evolutionary and ancestral health, I could explore any medical topic through this critical lens and would never just memorize biochemical enzymes or drug names. Learning about a drug was a gateway to understanding why the problem for which the drug was employed might have developed in the first place. Learning about biochemical enzymes was an opportunity to understand how various nutritional deficiencies affect the body and how those deficiencies clinically manifest. By viewing a patient's symptoms as how the body is trying to get back to normal instead of as the problems themselves, I could look at my patients and nearly everything I had to learn with radical curiosity.

What my classmates would categorize as a side effect of a drug to memorize, I would understand as a direct effect of a drug whose physiological underpinnings should be explored further so that the adverse effects could be limited or eliminated. What my classmates would observe as an interesting correlation between irritable bowel syndrome (IBS) and depression, I would understand as a potential causative relationship and an opportunity to explore the physiological and psychological roots of gut-brain disorders.

No matter how conflicting and upsetting certain aspects of the curriculum would be, I was the architect, the artist who would paint his own education even if all I had were a few colored highlighters.

Part II

Returning to It All

↢ 15 ↣

The Writer

Anatomy and the Musculoskeletal System: Take 2
January 2014

In preparation for my return to medical school, I spent more time with Thomas to discover how he had coped with the continued academic onslaught and, more importantly, how he made meaning outside of the classroom. Over much of the previous year, Thomas had sent out a weekly email known as the Mindfulness Practice Schedule to individuals interested in the pursuit of mindfulness. As a central figure connecting many of the seemingly disparate mindfulness communities around Charlottesville, he had amassed over three hundred email addresses from people looking for contemplative connection. With the help of then first-year student Athreya Tata, they rapidly grew the list and the ethos behind the messaging.

While Thomas continued to share his weekly email, Athreya and I brainstormed the beginnings of a new interdisciplinary student club to support self-discovery, resilience, and greater well-being. During the first few days of our formative and reflective work, Thomas suggested that we incorporate his weekly email into the club's evolving mission and, given his own excess of time commitments, that I specifically become the email's new writer. While I understood Thomas's rationale to bring his weekly newsletter within our developing student initiative, I couldn't help but stumble over the idea that I was to be its new author—was I ready to take this on?

I started my first email using his established framework of a short introductory message, words of gratitude from Gratefulness.org, a song, a photo, and the schedule of mindfulness events available to health sciences students and the Charlottesville community as a whole. Approaching the job as a nervous technician, I felt myself stepping back into the shoes of the eager but uncertain researcher I had been as I conducted my first reflective interview for the positive psychology research study. While crafting a message of compassion did not feel like a skill I readily possessed, I believed, with every ounce of my heart, that this was the most important use of my energy, my practice, and my time.

In January 2014, our student initiative Compassionate Awareness and Living Mindfully (CALM) was born, and my first Mindfulness Practice Schedule message made its way into email inboxes with its intention of gratitude, compassion, and love. With the first message sent, I stood at my desk as a backlog of tears ran down my cheeks. My frame—now over 130 pounds—slowly slipped backward to an open and inviting bed. With the welcome taste of salty joy, I closed my eyes to embrace every breath of an arising thought: healing was upon me and so, too, was my Sunday routine for the next three and a half years.

↜ 16 ↝

The Spiral

*Anatomy and the Musculoskeletal System: Take 2
February 2014*

By the end of the Musculoskeletal, Nervous System, and Anatomy module, I had passed all my exams and grown a close group of friends. The anatomy portion of the module was actually my third dissection of a cadaver as I had completed a full one before my leave the previous year and had even taken part in an anatomy class as an undergrad. As I entered the newly renovated lab one evening during my prep for the final cumulative exam, I was taken back in time to the scene just one year earlier—of the mentally destroyed, formaldehyde-coated shred of a student ready to swap places with the cadaver below his scalpel. I wanted to call back to that struggling past man and tell him that he was loved, he was cared for, and he would eventually find his way.

I mean, in what universe could I have imagined stopping school and going to a hospital where I would begin a yoga and meditation practice, discover the world of podcasts and integrative health, start work as a research assistant in a positive psychology research study, make an unexpected dear friend, attend a yoga research conference, start a group called CALM focused on growing medical student wellness, and then find myself back in the anatomy lab in an identical gown and gloves, but with a wholly transformed perspective?

I used to describe 2013 as the "circular miracle," but I have since come to see that what I once perceived as a circular path was actually an ascending spiral with a journey that would include constant revisitations to the same themes, people, and relationships.

The anatomy final was ultimately canceled because of a school closure for heavy snow. We got a few feet over the course of multiple weeks that winter, and I once again found myself walking the same hills with inches of snow beneath my feet—except this time, I did not consider stopping, sleeping, or leaving this world behind.

17

Small World Love

Mind, Brain, and Behavior: Neurology and Psychology
March 2014

As I had missed out on the critical social orientation with my new classmates, I faced an uphill battle to make new friends in the bustle of school. One weekend, I decided to change up my study routine and go to the Learning Studio, one of the main lecture and study areas of our medical school. While I assumed that the Learning Studio would be empty and quiet, I also knew that I would not meet anyone in my own room. When I got there, however, I saw one person studying away inside. As I neared her table, I noticed that she was wearing a Davidson College sweatshirt. Many of you have likely heard of Davidson because of arguably its most famous alumnus, the basketball star Stephen Curry, but the college itself is a very small school in North Carolina with few outside of the town aware of its existence.

For me, Davidson, while not my alma mater, was essentially where I grew up. My father's parents had moved to Davidson in the 1960s when my grandfather got a job at the college as an English professor. Growing roots in the small community, my grandparents never left, and my father met my eventual mother just a few miles away in a nearby town called Huntersville. From Christmas and Easter and long stretches of summer, Davidson and the surrounding area had become a second home for my brother and me, and if not for the private school tuition, would have been my home for college just a few years before.

As she looked up from her computer, she greeted me with a joyful smile.

I nervously hurried to get the first word in.

"I like your sweatshirt. My grandparents live there, and it's a beautiful town."

"Oh, how cool! I loved going to college there!" she exclaimed, her eyes meeting mine.

Losing myself a little as I saw how attractive she was, I stumbled into a new sentence.

"Are you a first-year?" I asked.

"Yes, and you?"

"Technically I started with the 2016 class, but I took some time off and now I'm restarting with you. I'm Rob."

"I'm Juliana. Nice to meet you!"

Besides being wickedly smart, I learned that Juliana had been a swimmer at Davidson and had even gone to a private high school in the same athletic conference as my own. She was also in my college at the medical school— one of four the school used to divide students into functional academic cohorts. I was guaranteed to see a lot of Juliana in the coming clinical years.

We finished talking, and I sat down next to her to study. Perhaps I wouldn't have to be alone on this journey. Perhaps I could do medical school differently after all.

⁓ 18 ⁓

The Deception of Control

Psychotherapy—High Street
May 2014

The first months back in medical school went by in an instant as my new study techniques and positive outlook powered me through test after test. While no student would say they strolled through medical school, I would be lying if I said that my most challenging work during those first months back took place inside of medical school walls.

After my initial rehabilitation at UNC, I returned to Charlottesville with a new interdisciplinary medical team. Led by the primary care clinician who had initially evaluated me on that fateful day in early February 2013, my medical team also included a psychotherapist and a dietitian. While my work with the dietitian felt a bit futile because of my evolving understanding of my own nutritional needs that were in stark contrast to the dietitian's knowledge base, my relationship with the psychotherapist emerged as one with deep potential. Together, we built on the foundation I'd laid with my therapist at UNC, unearthing the wounds that cried out for deeper love.

While the first few months of our work were primarily about empathetic support as the therapist listened and received what I brought to the sessions, she eventually asserted some direction for our relationship. While I did not fully understand the why behind many of her questions, we meandered back through time to explore the roots of my medical school unraveling. Although I now understood my relationship to achievement, I'd yet to delve into my anxieties around control and loss.

For twenty-four years I had lived as a twin, with a fraternal brother just two minutes younger than I was. Inseparable until college, my brother and I were alternately close and distant as we struggled to find our way after we'd left home. While we both knew we would attend different colleges, I didn't appreciate the magnitude of the separation until long after the split itself.

Once in college, I dove into a new world with new friends, new explorations, and unfathomable possibilities. Days into freshman orientation, during an activity between different dorms, I met an attractive and quirky woman who grabbed my attention. Skinny like myself with an infectious boat of sarcasm, we eventually embarked on a relationship.

Over the months of freshman year, our intimacy evolved, moving through stages of growth and peculiar unknowing. Into our second semester of school, however, I sensed a change in the air, an unsettled sensation of just how little I knew. Eventually our relationship ended, and it felt like death.

What in the world had I done wrong, and why had this failed?

Amid this crumbling there was also another slow fire building—a spark of self-loathing I had yet to fully acknowledge.

While I had experienced the normal teenage acne, my freshman year of college brought out an entirely new beast. With my face increasingly disfigured and my body equally so, I convinced myself that my unattractiveness was what had ended my relationship and started to obsess over improving my physical appearance.

Despite my growing attention, my skin got worse and worse through the spring of 2009. I got dressed in the dark and stopped looking in the mirror, unable to bear witness to my appearance to the world. In the middle of this growing self-disgust and desire to escape, my grandmother was diagnosed with metastatic cancer. Her prognosis worsened, and her days became fewer.

While I had planned to spend the summer of 2009 on the Appalachian Trail with my dear friend Max, I needed to see my grandmother before her passing.

In an effort to speed up my visit with her and my escape into the wilderness with Max, I took all five of my college finals in three days. Alone in a desolate room in the mathematics building, I cried over a Calculus III exam. This would be the first exam I would ever fail. While the idea of failing had been a sarcastic joke among my overachieving high school friends, in this moment, I couldn't answer many of the questions on my final exam. Failure and loss would be inevitable.

After I completed the exams, Max and I made our way to my grandparents' house. Inside the simple home in which I had spent so many summers, I welcomed my grandmother's glowing faith in the face of her transition onward.

"I can't lose this one, Rob. Either I get a few more weeks here on Earth or I get to go be with the Lord. Definitely beats losing to your brother and grandpa in canasta."

I was reluctant to leave her in such a precarious physical state, but she assured me she was in God's hands and thanked me for coming to visit her in this final chapter of life.

Eventually we left my grandmother to her unyielding faith and made our way to the mountains of North Georgia. Beginning at Springer Mountain, Max and I set out on our summer adventure. Carrying everything we needed in our Osprey backpacks, we coursed north on the AT into North Carolina and Tennessee. While we took in the amazing scenery of the Smoky Mountains and embraced the monotony of the beloved "green tunnel," I could not ignore my grandmother's declining health and my own health issues that were not disappearing in the seclusion of the woods.

Just weeks after Max and I ended our walk on a random highway in Tennessee, my grandmother passed away. Joining my loved ones in a celebration of her life, I gradually made peace with her passage to another place beyond. While I rested in the remembrance of my grandmother's care and love and reminisced about the miles of scenic trail walked with my dear friend Max, my acne and allergies continually dragged me back from this place of relative tranquility into a world of despair and unrelenting self-loathing.

The seeds of my path as a healer were slowly being planted, sown in the soil of my own unraveling. Healers don't become healers tending to other people's wounds; healers become healers because they walk through their own fall.

19

"Side Effects"

College of William and Mary
Summer 2009–Summer 2010

After I returned to college for my second semester, my skin was well on its way to healing. With the use of a powerful medication known as Accutane, my skin went through one more eruption before it began to find calm. By early fall 2009, I was no longer preoccupied with my "disfigurement," but the residue of my acne's trauma to my sense of self had not been healed with the sloughing of keratinocytes.

Since I suspected that the college cafeteria food had played a role in my worsening skin the year before, I became more cautious about what I consumed. As I ate less and less of the cafeteria food, I tried to find the particular culprits behind my skin's destruction. I landed on the idea that certain fats and refined foods were likely the cause. While refined foods certainly played a central role, the idea that fat was the enemy was, well, just plain wrong.

As I became stricter about my food, I began to ride my bicycle around the slow hills of Williamsburg. Combined with the miles I would walk around campus and my time at work in the Apollo's Chariot games area of the Busch Gardens Europe theme park, I burned around 3,500 calories a day. Despite consuming multiple meals and snacks, I started to lose weight from a frame of around 130 pounds. The problem? I had stopped looking in mirrors to observe my physical appearance, and my mind was slowly entering a state of isolation, restlessness, and an insidious loss of control.

Accutane, the powerful medication used to treat severe acne, is a peculiar substance. Known generically as isotretinoin, it is a synthetic form of retinoic acid, a biologically active form of vitamin A. While its mechanism of action has been debated for years, more recent research has pointed to one possible underlying pathway: the induction of apoptosis. *Apoptosis* is the biological term for programmed cell death, essentially the controlled destruction of an individual cell. Through apoptosis, surrounding cells not undergoing cell death are protected from the unnecessary inflammation that would occur if the cell underwent a much more traumatic and unplanned death pathway known as *necrosis*. How would telling certain cells to die improve acne? It all depends on which cells are getting the apoptotic signal.

One of the central features of acne is the dysregulated production of sebum, an oily type of substance produced from cells called sebocytes. Doctors recognize that hormones like testosterone stimulate sebocytes and puberty-ravaged teenagers and women with higher testosterone levels display greater levels of acne. While a root cause medical approach recognizes that sebum itself can't be the issue—as sebum is a critical part of the skin barrier and immune system—traditional medicine loves to find drugs that inhibit dysregulated pathways or drugs that inhibit the overproduction of substances that *seem* like the root issue.

This is precisely what Accutane does.

With the induction of sebocyte apoptosis, the body experiences a drastic reduction in sebum production alongside significant changes in the turnover of skin cells that result, over time, in a decreased number of acne lesions. Before we call Accutane a miracle drug, I will point out one other critical fact about this drug—and essentially all other drugs for that matter. The therapeutic mechanism of action of Accutane, the induction of apoptosis in sebocytes, is not the only effect this medication can possibly have.

There are *no* medicines that can be injected, inhaled, swallowed, or intravenously delivered that *only* provide the desired therapeutic effect for the dysregulated cells/tissues of interest. While most people likely understand this concept at the extremes—such as with chemotherapy that kills millions of cells throughout the body, both cancerous and noncancerous, and causes hair loss, ulcers, and anemia among many other problems—we are much less aware of the nontherapeutic effects of drugs when they are rather mild. Popularly known as side effects, these nontherapeutic effects have been framed by pharmaceutical companies and doctors alike as seemingly random and unpredictable events.

This is a flat-out lie.

Side effects occur in *all* patients taking a medication because side effects are simply a *function* of what the medication does.

For some individuals, the degree of a medicine's nontherapeutic effects is so minimal that they don't manifest as an overt or functionally limiting symptom. In this scenario, it would seem that the person did not actually have any side effects, but the truth is this person has experienced the therapeutic effects of the drug alongside its nontherapeutic effects, but given their individual systems of drug elimination, detoxification, and the nature of the drug itself, the body did not experience enough cellular dysfunction for such symptoms to noticeably manifest.

As an example, most drugs are eliminated from the body after being metabolized in some fashion by the liver and its host of specialized enzymes. With modern advancements in genomic medicine, we now recognize significant genetic variations in how quickly and robustly certain sets of these enzymes function in various individuals. One person may have a very robust system of enzymes to metabolize Drug A, but not Drug B, while another person may have the exact opposite pattern of genetic expression around these drug-metabolizing enzymes. If the first person with a less robust set of enzymes to metabolize Drug B actually takes Drug B, they will have higher levels of Drug B in their system for a longer period of time as compared to another person with a more robust set of metabolizing enzymes for Drug B. With Drug B circulating at higher levels and for a longer period of time, the individual has an increased potential to experience more cellular effects, both therapeutic and nontherapeutic. Expanding this scenario to days, weeks, months, and even years of taking Drug B, we can start to see cumulative increases in nontherapeutic effects, often alongside decreases in therapeutic effects, as the body adapts to the changes induced by the medicine.

Does it start to make sense now how one person could have greater levels of nontherapeutic effects from a medicine than another and how the accumulation of nontherapeutic effects at a cellular level can build over time to actually manifest as a clinically noticeable symptom or side effect?

When we look at Accutane, we see that it induces apoptosis in more cells than just sebocytes. In addition to sebocytes, research suggests that Accutane can induce apoptosis in neural crest cells, a key developmental cell in a young fetus. Because of this nontherapeutic effect, Accutane is considered a teratogenic medication and cannot be given to pregnant women under any circumstance. Accutane has also been found to induce apoptosis in certain brain cells in the hippocampus, lowering neurogenesis or new neuron cell development. Many clinicians have theorized that decreased neurogenesis is a cellular mechanism behind the observation of increased clinical depression and suicidality in some individuals taking Accutane despite improvements in their acne and skin appearance. In addition to these potential deleterious effects, Accutane has been shown to induce apoptosis in muscle cells, liver cells, cells of the hair follicle/sebaceous unit, intestinal cells, and perhaps even cancerous cells.

This is how drugs *actually* work. They affect cells in multiple tissues, providing various degrees of therapeutic or nontherapeutic effects that may or may not result in a net therapeutic benefit or the appearance of a noticeable side effect. Despite these undeniable facts of biology and pharmacology, most of the public and even clinicians grossly overestimate benefits of medications and underestimate their potential harms.

For me, the dermatologist who prescribed me Accutane likely felt like a lifesaver, and in some ways he was. Over several months, I went from acne over almost my entire body to essentially no acne whatsoever. At the same time, however, I became more restless, isolated, and stuck in a state of mental agitation. I cannot prove to you that Accutane was the cause of this mental shift—and it most certainly couldn't have been the only factor at play—but the Accutane certainly exerted antitherapeutic effects and my life was not entirely blissful in the months after treatment despite my being essentially acne-free.

While I can look back with sadness at my isolated and confused self, lacking either self-confidence or an enduring sense of well-being despite my improved skin, I only feel an odd sense of undeniable gratitude for my emerging unraveling. Without that fall, I would never have found my way.

… 20 …

Weaving the Story

Psychotherapy—High Street
May 2014

As I sat on my psychotherapist's couch, the whole story began to come together. Starting with the perceived loss of my brother as I entered college, I traced loss after loss and the resulting need for control. From losing a girlfriend to losing my self-confidence because of the severe acne to losing my grandmother and my roommate of two years, it felt like all I could do was lose. The world was a threatening place, and I needed to protect myself from more losses.

After the spring semester of 2009 and my worst academic performance as a student, I resolved to do better, and better I certainly would do. Through my sophomore year, my efforts at control and loss prevention became exacting. From athletic pursuits and schoolwork to my nutritional intake and work schedule, rigidity and I woke to the same sun.

During one of our most poignant sessions, my psychotherapist held my eyes as I cried for the younger version of me, shielding himself with the heavy armor of achievement. I cried for the young man who ignored his physical form, his world a state of perpetual agitation with sleep only a temporary respite. I cried for the person who was simply searching unknowingly for the divine within himself and the world.

Week after week I walked the mile or so from my apartment to the therapist's office. I looked forward to the sessions, even if I felt pain and guilt and cried. I wove a story from those fragmented, agitated years. I understood now that I needed rest, freedom, and love.

In her book, *Choosing Wisdom*, Dr. Margaret Plews-Ogan speaks frequently about the "personal narrative" or more simply put "the story of who we are." She describes this as a tapestry where individual parts of our lives and how we perceive them are constantly woven in as threads. As an example, someone can see a child congratulate another student for doing well on a test and weave the thread that "the world is full of gratitude" into their tapestry. Another can take that same objective experience and weave the thread that "achievement brings your recognition and love." Two individuals can take the exact same threads of experience and weave profoundly different tapestries of meaning reflecting their perceptive state of being. Just as one artist can be rendered helpless by a spilled blotch of paint on a masterpiece, another can turn that accident of color into something more meaningful than any of the purposeful strokes that came before it. We create our own unique tapestries even if we are all using the same threads.

The success of any therapy or healing approach rests in the therapy's ability to lead you back lovingly toward a deeper knowing of yourself—the tapestry of who you are. Paradoxically, to reach this state of knowing you must first undergo the process of unknowing and let go and rework the threads that block you from the present moment and the truth of who you really are.

I was getting my first lesson in weaving, and I would never need a loom.

21

Family Travels

Italy
July 2014

I have been blessed throughout my life with the ability to travel. My family has always valued experiences and travel over anything tangible, and we had made regular trips every two or so years with my extended kin to various national and international destinations. From Costa Rica and the Galápagos to England and Alaska, we have traveled significantly and with a purpose of seeing the world.

After I finished the spring semester of medical school in early May, I traveled to Buckingham, Virginia, for an initial period of study as part of an intensive yoga teacher training with the American Viniyoga Institute and its founder Gary Kraftsow. After two weeks of immersion into the therapeutic applications of yoga and the positive reconstruction of my own personal practice, I flew to Italy to join my family on another of our explorations.

While we spent most of our time as a family at a lovely villa, we made day trips to many of the surrounding areas and rented bikes to ride through the countryside and bask in it all.

Before this trip, I had significantly curtailed my biking. Being on the bike after my return from the hospital became antitherapeutic, inducing a fear that I could not ride it safely because it might just become my escape again from the feelings I did not want to fully embrace. Now in Italy, far away from my medical school obligations, my fear, anxiety, and past losses melted away as the European hills whispered back to me that everything would be okay.

During one of our many rides, we got caught in a monster of a thunderstorm. With lightning flashing across the darkened sky, I witnessed the full force of my repressed emotions acted out in the theater that was Mother Nature. With the sky as black as our curvy roads, rain pelted our bodies and the headwind made forward progress almost impossible. As I began to shiver in the sudden cold, I stepped off my bike and looked for the leading edge of the storm.

Despite my apparent openness during my first year of healing, I often wanted to erase the hospital and wipe out the image of the helpless young man who had driven himself into oblivion. I didn't want people to know how sick I had once been.

Can't I just show to the world the "new" me without the faintest hint of what I was before my breaking?

As the storm abated, the sky began to clear and light reemerged across the Tuscan hills. Warming the road and my body almost instantaneously, the sun caressed away my goose bumps, and I wiped away the last of the fallen rain from my brow. By tomorrow morning, the road would be dry and crisp, and even the collected puddles would be on their way to becoming veins of a carved Earth.

Children love puddles.

Perhaps it was time I started loving puddles, too.

~ 22 ~

A Student for Love

Cardiology and Nephrology
August 2014

After I returned from my last summer vacation as a student, I jumped back into the routine I had come to rather enjoy. With five months of preclinical school remaining, I needed to create a plan for the first in a series of board exams medical students and young physicians must pass in order to become licensed doctors. At this point, I had amassed a decent working knowledge of the innumerable medical topics I had explored to date. The challenge of medical school, however, is not learning and reciting newly absorbed knowledge in the moment, but rather retaining and integrating what you've learned into a working narrative that ultimately allows you to walk alongside patients in their efforts to heal.

One afternoon during another day of studious ennui, I stumbled across a program called Firecracker. A visionary adaptive learning program for medical students, Firecracker utilizes specialized question banks and algorithms to help you learn material you've struggled to retain. Just three questions into my first question bank, I felt an inarticulate joy that I had just found the holy grail for medical students, exponentially increasing my retention of the rigorous curriculum. With this one tool alone, I could study for my first board exam, three hours a day over a period of six months, and completely forgo the stressful cramming period that typically awaited students before the dreaded exam itself.

I realize that many of you are likely wondering again, *what is so interesting about how you studied in medical school?* I get it—these stories, like the ones that came before it, could have been pushed aside and completely off the page, but these methods and the time they represent are just as much a part of me as my time in yoga teacher training, my time traveling in Italy, or my hours of reflection in the positive psychology research study. If anything, the stories about my study habits are *more* a part of my everyday reality and the realities of my medical school peers than anything else. Social media would love for us to believe in the edited world we collectively showcase, but the truth behind all those filtered images is often much rawer and more brutal. Because I was a professional student, my job was to be ruthless in my critical acquisition of knowledge and, at the same time, loving to myself and my peers. Wasting time with poor study habits or utilizing distracting technology would only lead to greater suffering and invariably less collective love.

My goal for acquiring efficiency was not efficiency for financial gain or for efficiency's sake. My goal was to increase my capacity to love others while I made space to fully love and care for myself.

23

The End of the Beginning

I-64 East
December 2014

After completing my last preclinical exam, I pointed my Toyota RAV4 toward home for an extended holiday break. As my iPod shuffled through various Christian artists, the rhythm of each song reached out to match the beat of my own heart. Wrapped in this melodious calm, I was suddenly hit by a mixture of elation, surprise, fear, and disbelief. I pulled over to the side of the road as tears started to run down my cheeks and chin and onto my sweater and jeans.

While I only knew fifteen to twenty people on the CALM email list of over three hundred, I felt connected and entrusted by this community to shine a light of awareness and reflective truth so that we could all flourish in our respective acts of self and communal love.

Now, here I was, on a deserted interstate in the middle of central Virginia with hours to go until I could slip into my childhood bed. My tears had nearly washed out my contacts, and my heart raced from a symphony of released hormones. I turned off my iPod and sat in silence with the surrounding night. Taking note of my deepening breath, I closed my eyes and felt myself connecting with this most peculiar of meditative cushions. Slipping back to feel the soft buttress of its accompanying headrest, my darkened visual field provided a means to focus on images of my relatively unknown community. Visualizing scenes of children and the aging wise, I "watched" in wonder as they moved to form a half circle and face my state of perceiving awareness.

"We see you, darling, as you desire to see us."

As I watched them softly bow in reverent gratitude, my visual field flooded again with darkness, and I opened my eyes to the remnants of my erupted tears.

The world can be your meditation cushion if you let it—cupholders and all.

← 24 →

How We Lost Our Way

Chesapeake, Virginia
January 2015

I had been home with my parents for just over a month, and my routine while home involved walks in nature, regularly scheduled meals, and hours of preparatory questions and test simulations for my upcoming USMLE Step 1 Exam, the first of several examinations required for the continuation and completion of medical training. For whatever silly reason, USMLE Step 1 had turned into a monster, taking on an undeserved degree of importance for later residency applications as it ground down preclinical medical students into soulless fragments of themselves, gripped by the fear that one standardized test could decide their professional future.

Designed to be taken after the preclinical years, Step 1 includes questions to assess a vast array of medical knowledge, but with a heightened focus on foundational concepts learned prior to any formal time in clinical settings. Like many standardized tests, deciding what is of significant value to be included on Step 1 and how to precisely quantify a candidate's knowledge of the material remains contentious. While arguments have and will be made on all sides regarding the content and grading of this test, its greatest injustices and issues, in my opinion, involve its question design and its disproportionate focus on rare and uncommon disease processes.

There is a saying in medicine (and I would think many versions) that when you are seeking to diagnose or identify a specific disease process, you should not go looking for zebras when you live on a horse ranch. While medicine is full of obscure and rare conditions we like to call "zebras," the majority of medicine is full of common, well-described patterns that fill up our "horse ranch." You would think that standardized tests would ask questions on topics in proportion to their presence and overall relevance in the field—more questions about horses and less about zebras—but USMLE Step 1 is not that kind of test. From questions about rare immunodeficiency and glycogen storage conditions to what type of glycoproteins are present in certain viruses, the test is full of material that will be clinically relevant to only a small percent of future physicians. Sounds like a great way to figure out who will be an accomplished physician, doesn't it?

While I could make an argument that the test's disproportionate focus on rare and uncommon disease processes is its biggest issue, the test's most insidious and problematic issue is its reliance on multiple-choice questions that ask you to pick the best or "most correct" answer. While this type of question design is common both within and outside of medical education, it has become a subject of many memes and consistent jokes generated by both medical and nursing students who have been burned one too many times by picking an answer that was technically correct, but just not the best one. One of my favorite memes regarding these types of test questions involves a picture of four identical oranges with the caption, *"Which of these is the most orange?"* You get the picture.

Interestingly, while testing in medical education seems to have no issue living in the "land of the gray," the practice of clinical medicine and our interpretation of disease somehow has become strictly dichotomous with individuals either having or not having a disease, being sick or not sick from a certain ailment, being a candidate for a diagnostic test or being told it's wasteful. While doctors like things to be black and white in the decision-making process, the practice of medicine and helping humans achieve well-being are anything but.

Testing and learning methodology in our medical schools may emphasize the wider perspective, the multifactorial, and the unexplainable, but as soon as you get into clinical practice, medical decisions become either right or wrong, applicable or not applicable, gold standard or quackery.

Where in the world did we go wrong?

While I can't even attempt to give you an abbreviated answer to that question, I *can* tell you how this question and many others crashed through my mind as I sat in hour five of my USMLE Step 1 Exam. As I read through a question about high blood pressure and what would be an appropriate medication for someone with chronic kidney disease and high potassium levels, I couldn't help but ask: How did we get here? *Even if we need a medication, why can't food also be an answer?* In nearly every block of questions, I confronted a "correct" test answer that was completely different from my beliefs and choices in real life. What is a reasonable medication for someone with mild depression worried about sexual side effects? *Sure, I have a guess for you, but who says they need medication in the first place?* For someone with uncontrolled diabetes on two medications, what would be a safe third medication to add? I have an answer for that, *but where is there an option for dietary modification?* As I answered question after question about pathophysiology and chronic disease, I couldn't help but ask what dysfunctional aspect of a person's lifestyle or tragic life circumstance got them here in the first place?

Prior to the test, I had trained by replicating the testing environment in terms of the total questions I would see in a certain allotment of time. Outside of these preparations, I also spent a great deal of mental energy to silence the dissonance the test would create. I would have to play "their" game, by "their" rules, and give "their" answers, not mine. Despite this preparation, as I sat in my oversized computer chair with noise-canceling headphones, I was struck over and over again by what exactly had been deemed worthy for this test.

Is this really what our medical education system and doctors have become? Is this what we need to learn in order to walk alongside patients in their healing journeys?

After I answered the final question of the eight-hour USMLE Step 1 adventure, I stood up, collected my things, and made my way back to my RAV4 so that I could sit in reflective silence to honor my efforts and my hours of curious inquiry. While the transition to clinical care was still weeks away, it had become exceedingly clear from a random selection of computer-generated questions that I was not here to study drug mechanisms, disease syndromes, or rare immunodeficiency pathologies. I was not even here to study lifestyle treatments for chronic disease. I was here to study *the human experience*. No matter the disease state or objective data, I was here to understand people's experience of life, sickness, and the maintenance of their health and, through it all, to explore how we all could lose our way.

Beyond the Blade

General Surgery
March 2015

As if God knew what I needed to instill my resolve, I began my third year of medical school—my first year of rigorous clinical education beyond the classroom—with a twelve-week clinical rotation in general and specialized surgery. For third-year medical students, beginning clinical rotations is something akin to swimming for the first time without a life jacket, floaties, or a mom's hands at the ready. While any first rotation for a third-year student involves a massive transition—both in life and academic routine—there is probably none greater than the transition into surgery.

The surgical arena with its operating rooms, postanesthesia units, and even the postsurgical hospital ward is a downright alien environment. Behind every mask and apron, behind every scalpel and cautery device are minds and hands all at work seeking to provide a net benefit to the patient by the targeted intoxication and destruction of tissue. Surgery has come a long way, and it's easy to forget in our technological age where things began. But thanks to many, including the well-known Dr. Atul

Gawande, the process of all surgeries has become strategically ritualized and focused on the minimization of risk.

As I finished my first hand-scrubbing, I couldn't help but feel, no matter how minuscule my involvement in the operating room would be, that for there to be a net benefit for the patient, it would be best for me to simply greet them with a large smile after they woke up from anesthesia. While my mind screamed out to get as far away as possible from this unknown world, my heart opened to embrace the uncertainty, the uncontrollable, and the present moment beckoning me.

While I wanted to pursue a career in family and integrative medicine, my surgical rotation offered an unexplainable gift: an opportunity to observe the entire process of surgery, from start to finish, without a compulsion to hyperfocus on the role of the surgeon alone. Attentive to the anatomy and the process, but not transfixed by the scalpel, I saw opportunities to work with the anesthesiologist preoperatively where I could meet the patient and even explore some of the fears and concerns they were experiencing. I could walk back with patients in their hospital bed and observe the targeted transitions employed by the multiple surgical techs and aides. I could bear witness to the organization of the main surgical assistant, the checklist and the time-out conducted by the head nurse. I could see the still "new" hands of the resident surgeon, accomplished but raw to the specific technique and desires of the attending surgeon. I could notice the heartbeat, the temperature, and oxygen saturation. I could watch with a laparoscopic camera in hand as the aorta pulsed and pulsed away. I could walk with patients as they roused in the postanesthesia unit, and be by the bedside on the postoperative floor as the healing continued to progress. I could talk with nurses and aides, techs and respiratory therapists, residents and fellows and, of course, the patients themselves.

While we can see the surgeons as the lifesavers, the essential personnel providing services to restore the ailing body, surgery is a team sport. We need the orchestra behind the violin, the center fielder behind the pitcher, the love behind the blade. Which then begs the question:

How much blade do we really need?

The world will never stop needing surgeons, but it certainly could have them work a lot less often. Between my rotations on general, orthopedic, endocrine, and thoracic surgery, I saw organs from gallbladders and appendixes to thyroids, thymuses, and full lobes of the lung removed because of "irreparable" maladies. From cancer and hyperthyroidism to gallstones, inflamed appendixes, carpal tunnel, and autoimmune disease, the surgeons were ready and able to remove pathologic tissue and seek some semblance of restoration for the patient at hand. With every specimen collected and sent, I asked, *where did this go wrong?* From obesity and smoking to apparently the purely genetic and the famously idiopathic, the reasons for surgery were grossly inadequate.

How could this have been avoided? Where did the patient lose their way?

We will always need surgeons, but with a healthy population, how much surgery would we need? With a nonsmoking population, how much lung cancer requiring lobectomy would there be? With a nonobese population how many gallbladders and cancers would ever require removal? With massive taxes on sugar-sweetened beverages and cigarettes, how much easier could it be for someone to avoid these problematic substances? With employer incentives to pursue physical activity and receive preventative lab work, how many more healthy workers could we create and support? With the employment of radical price transparency and the reformation of a broken healthcare system, how many people could we help avoid bankruptcy from medical bills?

These are the tough questions we have to start asking as a whole, and it was radically apparent to me, even in my early days as a third-year student, that we were actively creating a self-destructive environment and, in many cases, simply rearranging the deck chairs on the *Titanic*. The way through involves more rearranging and more sinking; the way beyond involves acknowledging and addressing the icebergs beneath the surface that are our own self-destructive creations.

~ 26 ~

Irony

Thoracic Surgery
May 2015

I was in the last stretch of my surgery rotation and needed to complete just three more weeks with the thoracic surgeons. Feeling more comfortable in the operating room and postoperative floor, I was now less a fish out of water and just a fish in water too cold for its liking. The daily routine of waking shortly after 4 a.m. to dress and walk to the hospital for pre-rounding was, dare I say, a comfortable one. While I had no time for sitting meditation given these early hours, my morning walk in the cool spring air, still bathing in the soft light of the stars high above, became its own meditation—a preparation and a prayer for those I would care for over the course of the day. With barely a soul awake, as even the last of the college students had turned in after 2 a.m., the walk was as serene as it could be for someone headed to an operating room in which he wanted no part.

During my early-morning review of the preoperative list that included our patients and their respective procedures, I felt an odd sinking in my stomach, a sense that today was not going to be an ordinary day. Once at the hospital, I found the surgical resident and completed our pre-rounding duties. From there, I moved to the operating room, where I greeted the thoracic surgery fellow so we could discuss the first case. Equipped with student intel about the thoracic surgery fellow's demeanor and demands, I was prepared to deal with someone who had little patience for medical students and wanted to have finished his training yesterday.

While we can't excuse anyone's rude and toxic attitude, I understood why he acted the way he did. With less than a month remaining in his formal training—a journey that had included four years of medical school followed by five years of general surgery residency and two years of specific training in thoracic surgery—his cynicism and frustration for medical students and the system as a whole were not a surprise. I'd be hard-pressed to imagine anyone walking that journey and getting so close without cynicism and frustration. We can blame the broken and ignore the system that broke them, but this only leads to more breaking.

On paper, our first case sounded like a chance at a heroic cure. The patient was a woman with a rare neuromuscular autoimmune condition called myasthenia gravis. As part of the condition, many individuals develop abnormal growth of the thymus, an interesting little organ that sits in the upper portion of the thoracic cavity between the two lungs. The thymus is the primary maturation site for an immune cell known as a T cell. These T cells come in many different flavors, but in general, they are responsible for orchestrating the adaptive or targeted immune response. In some instances, however, T cell function can become dysregulated and these same T cells can inadvertently recognize or damage our own tissues as part of an autoimmune reaction or disease. In the case of myasthenia gravis, researchers had identified antibodies to multiple components of the neuromuscular junction, the functional unit for initiating muscular contractions. Because of these antibodies and the larger dysregulated immune response, individuals with myasthenia gravis get fatigued easily and often develop baseline weakness across several muscle groups. In an effort to stop the dysregulated immune response and the abnormal thymus growth, surgeons had started to remove the thymus and found that some individuals experienced an improved disease course with fewer symptoms.

The patient, a sweet, obese woman in her late sixties, was a grandmother and had suffered from symptoms related to myasthenia gravis for quite some time. As I talked to her in the pre-anesthesia unit and along our walk into the operating room, we quickly developed a bond.

Dear God, can this please go well?

Up until this point, my practice of prayer had been infrequent and scattered. On occasion, during the resting phases of my evening yoga practice, I would move into a state of reflective reverie and "receive" prayer from a state of relative silence. In this moment, however, I felt a growing urgency to speak with God as passive reception would not do.

As the surgery progressed, the surgeon uncovered a significant burden of fat and associated tissue that obscured normal anatomical landmarks and made it quite challenging to find the thymus tissue. We struggled for some time, and the attending surgeon became frustrated, with the thoracic surgery fellow not far behind. Throughout the procedure, I held the thoracoscopic camera—the window into the mediastinum that made a less invasive surgery possible. I had become acquainted with the use of the laparoscopic camera in the abdominal or peritoneal cavity as part of my time on the general surgery rotation a few weeks before, but today was the first time I had used such a camera in thoracic surgery and things were not going as well. Because of her girth, the placement of the thoracoscopic port, and the abundance of fatty tissue obscuring the organs we wanted to see, the camera would regularly get fogged and had to be removed and cleaned. While the distorting fog would be enough to make a surgeon's blood boil, I also possessed the beautiful skill of consistently directing the camera's lens to precisely the wrong place in the mind of the attending surgeon. As the "eyes of the surgeon," I was doing an inadequate job and the entire surgery was running raggedly downhill.

"You are the worst camera driver I've ever had," the attending surgeon finally blurted out.

"I am sorry, it's my first day in thoracic surgery."

I handed over the thoracoscopic camera to the fellow and took up a different role in the surgical arena. There was an eerie quiet in the room as no one spoke for the next several minutes.

Despite the change in camera operators, the visuals and the surgery did not improve. In the end, we never actually found a thymus. The fatty connective tissue that was excised, perhaps containing some thymic tissue, was accidentally dropped on its way out of the body and couldn't be found within the mediastinal cavity even by the attending surgeon. Eventually, the surgery was called, the patient was sutured up, and we moved on to the next case.

The second case turned into another semidisaster with a patient that shouldn't have had surgery in the first place. We experienced significant trouble in removing major portions of the patient's lung, and I struggled to envision how this frail man could recover from such a challenging procedure.

The last surgery went smoothly although I never found out if the procedure actually helped the patient.

After completing my final student duties, I walked back home a little after 4 p.m. I had been awake and actively engaged in medical tasks for almost twelve hours. This was life as a medical student on surgery, and bedtime was quickly calling my name.

Two days later I found myself in the thoracic surgery clinic with the same attending surgeon. Without much pause or hesitation, the surgeon took me aside to talk.

"I want to apologize for what I said in the operating room two days ago. Those two surgeries were probably two of the toughest cases I have had in my entire career, and I appreciated you sticking with me to get through them."

It would be easy to look at those words as a scripted apology, but as the surgeon looked me in the eye, I felt a sincere desire for forgiveness.

"Thank you," I replied. "I am grateful for physicians like you who do the kind of work that I myself would never do."

The attending surgeon was one of the most accomplished general and thoracic surgeons in the hospital and in the country as a whole. While I have yet to use any descriptive pronouns in telling you this story, I wonder if you have pinned a specific gender on this attending surgeon anyway?

Does the phrase *attending surgeon* lead you to one particular gender?

How about the surgeon's outburst in the OR? Or did the apology change your mind?

No matter where you landed, the surgeon I have described to you is in fact a woman, a mother, and above all, a human.

Through this cognitive dance, we may see our predilection for creating understanding based on internal and often unconscious biases rather than described facts. We, as a whole, will often attribute feminine and masculine qualities as being male or female, despite the attribute or object having no such gender. In this way, we fail to see the difference between female and femininity, male and masculinity, and forget that every human, whether male or female, possess both feminine and masculine qualities.

In the field of medicine, where the majority of physicians are male, the style of medicine that is routinely practiced is decidedly paternalistic. While the rise of open access information has helped shift the style more toward shared decision-making, medicine is still heavily biased toward masculine drives and shrouded empathy. Female physicians often recognize the paternalistic style of education and practice and strive to fit in and survive. Paternalistic medicine is practiced by both men and women with the conformity to outdated healing systems remaining all too steadfast.

The future of medicine must be driven by an embracing of the feminine. In seeking balance between the necessary masculine and feminine qualities, our physicians, whether male or female, must come to grips with the need for action with receptivity, instruction with listening, stoicism with empathy, endurance with rest.

Medicine must engender a culture where both men and women are comfortable embracing and expressing such a mixture of qualities.

Our surgeon, despite her pursuit of a remarkably masculine profession, was still able to show the deep feminine qualities of connection, growth, and love, retaining the balance our healthcare workers most desperately need.

While I could end this story and this chapter with this conclusion, I would like to share one more miraculous story with you.

The surgeon, amid all of her research endeavors in the clinical and surgical setting, with over a hundred papers authored or coauthored, had chosen to be the primary investigator for the one study that had mattered more than anything in my life: the positive psychology study in cardiac surgery patients. During the interactions I've just described, she had no idea that the medical student with whom she had become so irate and to whom she eventually shared a heartfelt apology was actually the medical student who orchestrated a research study that bore her name.

27

"My Family"

Pediatrics
Summer 2015

My idea of friendship and family was as unorthodox as my approach to medicine. Over the two years since I had returned to school, my network of friends within the Charlottesville community grew into a fascinating melting pot. My friend George had become a second father to me. We regularly spent time together in the hospital to share our experiences of radically different worlds. Through him, I met most of the patient coordinating personnel and developed bonds with many in this tight-knit group. Within the school of nursing, I also continued to grow tremendous friendships. From nursing student and copresident of CALM, Jane Muir, to the dean of the Nursing School herself, Dorrie Fontaine, I relished these friendships between like-minded souls.

Within the medical school, however, my world remained fairly narrow. My closest friends included my previous roommate Thomas as well as my current roommates and previous classmates Nick Hac and Travis Halbert. In addition to my friendships with Juliana and Athreya, I developed close friendships with two other students in my new class, Karam and Kareem. Karam was the son of two Pakistani diplomats and lived far away from most of his family. While his older brother was also in the United States, he was essentially on his own without a car, trying to make it through school. Kareem was from Canada and perhaps the funniest guy in our entire class. From playing table tennis in the student lounge to complaining about something related to school, Kareem brought much-needed laughter to all of our lives.

Outside of school and the healthcare system entirely, I developed friendships in our local farmers market. Every Saturday morning from April through December, when I was not at the hospital, I walked from my apartment with my Osprey backpack and iPod Nano to a cleared-out parking lot in downtown Charlottesville to find the foods that nourished my soul. With my buddy Brian supplying me with more varieties of apples than I could count and my dear friend Corey who made sure I had the best spices to put on my food, I cherished these moments, rain or shine, to support the individuals who supported me.

Black, brown, and white; Christian, Buddhist, and Muslim; American, Canadian, and Pakistani; heterosexual, homosexual, bisexual; medical, nursing, and nonmedical—my world was a kaleidoscope of thought, religion, gender, occupation, ethnicity, and all the experiences that make up the human tapestry.

I have observed that it is common for humans to gravitate to those with shared beliefs and a similar appearance to find a sense of safety. At the same time, I have also noticed that humans gravitate to those with different beliefs and different appearances to deepen their felt experience of unified love. Love and safety are essential to flourish in this exceedingly complex world. Perhaps you will find them both when you have no hope at all.

≈ 28 ≈

The Poet

Charlottesville
Summer 2015

Despite my desire to find a partner, I had not been in a romantic relationship since my return to medical school. In all honesty, I hadn't been in a romantic relationship since my freshman year of college nearly seven years earlier. As part of the rigidity and habitual structure I had developed, I had little room for socialization, let alone a deeper relationship with another human being. Since early 2014, however, having made tremendous strides in my own healing and growing self-awareness, I felt ready for a new romantic relationship. While I was not in a hurry, I assumed it would be relatively easy to meet someone between my new medical school classes and my endeavors in mindfulness at the nursing school. Still, by early 2015, it had become clear that even this expanded sphere was still too narrow and every possibility was turning into a dead end.

One day a close friend shared her thoughts about online dating and dating apps. Some way into the conversation, she mentioned an app called Tinder founded on the idea of the "double opt-in," where individuals could each express interest in one another and know when there was a shared desire to pursue communication or a relationship.

Although I was initially exceedingly reluctant to try something that seemed so focused on judging physical appearance, I eventually decided I had nothing to lose as my social sphere would only get narrower as the third year of school churned ahead. During the long weeks of my surgery rotation in the middle of April, I matched with a few individuals on Tinder and started to have regular conversations with one woman in particular. Seemingly overnight, my evenings shifted from my previous academic routine to more social exploration, where my new friend Kelsey and I engaged in establishing an emerging connection. While she was from the Charlottesville area, Kelsey attended college in Roanoke, Virginia, and had interests in English, poetry, and the New England Patriots. Her personality was a unique blend of joyful bubbliness and sarcastic wit that was a great reprieve from my hours bathed in medical sterility and morbid cynicism. After a few weeks' worth of phone conversations and the completion of Kelsey's spring semester, we planned a first date at a local Starbucks. Even though I felt a sense of gentle ease with her presence during our evening calls, the suspense of our impending first in-person date created a curious degree of enthusiastic agitation.

How exactly do you show up to your first date in nearly seven years?

After I parked in the Starbucks parking lot, I found Kelsey and the smile I had only seen in pictures. We stepped inside to grab a couple of drinks and returned outdoors to enjoy the beautiful weather. Once seated, I looked into her eyes and felt my initial nervousness quickly fade away. In between sips of iced tea, I got up to speed with her family dynamics, her fascination with fungi, and her upcoming summer job working with some overexuberant goats. In between laughter and more sips of iced tea, we began to plan a summer of new adventures.

Outside of my clinical responsibilities and slow evenings with Kelsey, I continued to write the weekly Mindfulness Practice Schedule email. With each email delivered, I could feel my own metamorphosis from a nervous email technician into a more ambitious artist and conveyor of the human connection. In addition to the email, I started to write blog posts on a page I affectionately called "Rabbott Tracks." For someone who had managed to avoid taking a single English class in college, writing in several forms had surprisingly become a regular part of my life and had evolved into a critical practice that helped me to slow down and curiously explore my felt experience. In combination with my morning yoga practice, evening sitting meditation, and walks in nature, my writing efforts were part of a nonnegotiable set of well-being practices. In my hierarchy of pursuable activities, my well-being practices took precedence and got scheduled before any asynchronous school endeavors—and I mean any.

While my efficient study habits created more space for self-care and my writing, I viewed any margin of free time gained from such efficiency as surplus to devote to the nonnegotiable core. With each passing week in school, my surplus continued to grow. Resting with this unexpected contentment, I felt an unexpected and burgeoning desire to explore another form of writing and language altogether.

Poetry had been a part of my life since birth. Even when I was a pre-verbal child, poetry was shared in our family as a gift, an art form, the craft of my father's father. As I grew older, my grandfather's poems and writings made their way into my consciousness more noticeably as his books and collections passed in front of my eyes. Throughout middle and high school I dabbled in poetry as part of literature classes, but creative writing was not a regular pastime. In college and my early years of medical school, creative pursuits were essentially nonexistent while my world revolved around a scientific sun. As I started to spend more time in nature and in Kelsey's gentle presence, meandering through the simplest of paths and trails around my apartment in Charlottesville, I sensed an energetic awakening, an increased perception of the previously unseen. While my efforts with the blog and the Mindfulness Practice Schedule were certainly guided by a creative, curious intention, I always had a clear direction, an identifiable end result. What I unconsciously wanted, however, wasn't a blueprint or a deadline, a rubric or an outline—what I wanted was to simply listen for the words that had been passing over me for years and transcribe them in whatever ways I could.

Out on a local trail as I wandered across town, the words came as my feet strode along a leaf-covered path. Without much conscious thought, I brought out my iPhone and navigated to the Notes app. As I tapped away at the phone's excuse for a keyboard, I succumbed to the moment and simply prayed I wouldn't trip.

Photograph

What is a photograph, but a poem without words,
cursed without a voice, but blessed with the gift of light,
the colors dance upon my eyes,
and speak a different language.
Shadow, contours, reflections
all whispering in my ears
for it takes much more than silence
to keep a picture from speaking a thousand words.

Looking up from my cell phone screen, I stared at the greenery around me in relative disbelief. I had missed the last mile of trail and my neck was quite concerned about the sustainability of these creative wanderings.

Thank God for yoga.

The next morning I set back out into nature for another poetic cloud of rain. Battling early tendencies for incessant revision, I sent my first poem to Kelsey.
"'Rob, this is really wonderful! Thank you for sending it to me!"
"Already working on the next one. Get ready lol."
Day by day, my phone filled with more poems, photos of nature, and Kelsey's loving receptivity. Even on the most drudgerous of walks to the medical school, I found opportunities to write poems, undeterred by the suffering waiting on either side of the wander. Despite our relatively limited time together with my medical school requirements taking up so much space, my daily poems and ramblings brought continuity and growth to Kelsey's and my emerging relationship.

Ignited by an infamous dating app, spurred onward by daily poetry, and refreshed by deliveries of collected wildflowers, I found myself, once again, rewriting the rules of the game and resewing the tapestry that was my new walk at life.

∽ 29 ∽

The Armor

*Obstetrics, Emergency Medicine,
and Ambulatory Internal Medicine
August–September 2015*

After my experience in surgery, I moved on to a rotation that included time in obstetrics (OB) and gynecology. For the rotation I worked as part of a three-student group that included my first friend in my new medical school class, Juliana Porter. Juliana was arguably the quintessential physician in training. Embodying compassion with intelligence, discernment with faith, she was not only a friend but a role model in our efforts at medical service. She, like me, was a dedicated walker and was up in the early morning hours to make space for her own well-being practices before arriving first for any clinical duties.

With overlapping schedules that allowed Juliana and me to spend time together on the labor and delivery unit, we waited anxiously for new life to be brought into the world. A few days into the rotation and on one of our twelve-hour shifts, as we sought to try and find a home amid the bustle of the nursing staff, I began to see just how demanding Juliana was of herself and of her classmates.

"Are you going to be with the resident for the next delivery?" she blurted out.

"I think I am supposed to be in the next scheduled C-section," she continued with few spaces for breaths in between. "I just want to make sure the resident knows what we're doing and I don't miss anything. What were you planning to do?"

Unable to admit to my friend that any plan I would construct would involve walking miles away from the relative chaos of the labor and delivery unit, I calmly replied, "I will stay with the resident for the next vaginal delivery. Go help with the C-section, and I will let them know."

The next day, Juliana was still on the case.

"It looks like they rescheduled the workshop this afternoon. Should we go back to L&D? Do you think we should let them know?"

"I think it's going to be okay, Juliana. I was just planning to go home to spend some time reviewing material for the shelf exam," I replied with some growing exasperation.

"But what if they are expecting us now that things got rescheduled? I think we should go back or at least let them know."

"I am just going home, Juliana. I really think everything's going to be fine, but you are welcome to do whatever you want."

Realizing my desire to take advantage, rightly or wrongly, of this precious "found time," I collected my things and left Juliana with our third compatriot, Sarah. After I changed out of scrubs and stashed my white coat away in a small locker, I strapped my Osprey backpack over my shoulder and began the walk home. Before I could even untangle my headphones so that I could enjoy a podcast during my walk home, I felt a gnawing distress in my stomach.

Was I being a good student? Was I being a good friend?

Exasperated by the hectic environment of the labor and delivery unit, I had missed the real suffering and the real needs of my friend Juliana. With each step up the 14th Street hills, I saw more clearly the reflection of our shared humanity, my historical rigidity, and my own continued striving for my own way. Juliana was clearly distressed with the disruption in our schedule and the unclear expectations of her as a student. Within that uncertainty, she simply wanted to be well received by her friends and peers in order to find the stability and direction to move forward.

What is the real value of "found time" if in its pursuit you lose a friend?

The next day when I returned to the hospital I apologized to Juliana.
"I didn't mean to leave you guys and come across as not caring. I was tired and too focused on taking advantage of the free time."
"It's okay. You didn't need to apologize, but I appreciate you saying this to me. We actually both ended up going home, too, and it was nice to have a little break. I still can't believe we are almost halfway done with third year! We should try to get together at Sarah's house to celebrate when we're done with OB!" she exclaimed.

Over the next three weeks of our OB rotation, Juliana and I cultivated more moments as friends and sleep-deprived peers, and I found myself, in a bizarre turn of events, not wanting to leave OB and be separated from her. Despite this reluctance, I eventually followed the flow of the fire hydrant toward new rotations in internal medicine and emergency care.

While the month of July showered me with an unexpectedly positive experience on OB alongside more poems and nourishing time with Kelsey, the transition into August and my hours in the ER brought a decidedly different weather pattern. One evening, while I was walking to school for my third shift in the ER, I got a text from Kelsey.
"Hey Rob, this is really hard to say, but I think I need a little more space alone. I know you're busy and still want to be able to talk, but I'm not sure I will be up for doing much over the next couple of weeks."
"I understand, Kelsey. Take whatever space you need and please let me know if there's something I could do that would be helpful for you."
"Thanks, Rob. I really appreciate your messages and poems. I'll let you know if I am up for talking or a visit."
"Sounds good, baby. I'll be in the ER tonight. I'll message in the morning."
With just those few strokes on an iPhone keyboard, an emotional support I had come to rely on was starting to evaporate. Despite there being no objective change in my immediate surroundings and physical condition, I sensed an erupting emptiness in my stomach.

Was this the beginning of the end?

After I arrived at the ER, I joined my team to start the shift. Within minutes, I was staring at yet another electronic medical record in preparation to see a distressed ER patient and felt a hollow apathy I hadn't experienced for quite some time. While Kelsey and I had spent much of the summer in each other's company, even traveling to my family's lake property on a couple of occasions, her text had generated a degree of undesirable uncertainty I had not anticipated. Bouncing back and forth from this unstable future and the immediate demands of my ER shift, I recognized just how much I loathed the Emergency Room.

Continuing the cycle of reflective loathing, I suddenly realized that for most of the last three months, I had spent the majority of my time either in the surgical arena or on the labor and delivery unit—two places that did not match in the slightest with my personality or my goals to practice integrative medicine. Despite this front-loading of potential misery, I had made it to the final and shortest stop before ever feeling a weary load of apathy, all induced by the simple injection of relational uncertainty.

Just like no one thinks about an airplane seat cushion as a flotation device until the moment they need it, I had not recognized I was sitting on an emotional "life preserver" with my relationship until a few emergency lights came on to focus my attention.

"Nice joke, God! In the Emergency Room of all places."

While my "life preserver" was far more than just a good relationship with Kelsey—consisting of my different reflective practices, intentional writing, and time with friends as well—it took a disturbance in that relationship to finally see the tremendous impact of these nourishing endeavors.

How in the hell would I make it without these practices? How in the hell would I make it without dear friends?

As the final weeks of my ER rotation crawled by, I didn't hear from Kelsey, and I increasingly cringed under a growing burden of doubt. Following my time in the ER, I was scheduled to complete an outpatient medicine rotation known as Ambulatory Internal Medicine (AIM). Earlier that June I had chosen to be matched with an internal medicine physician in Roanoke so I could stay closer to Kelsey after she returned to school.

When I arrived in Roanoke, I texted Kelsey to let her know I had made it to the bed-and-breakfast where I'd be staying and shared my upcoming schedule of clinic days.

"Hey Rob! I'm just getting settled into a new routine here, too. Do you want to come over tomorrow night?"

"Definitely. Will be great to see you!"

The next evening, I drove over to Kelsey's apartment complex. Feeling welcomed by her joyful wit once again, we went inside to enjoy each other's company. As I updated her about my latest medical school adventures and the cute little B&B room I would have for the next few weeks, I felt the atmosphere thicken with what had been building for weeks.

"Rob, you are one of the kindest people I have ever known, and I have enjoyed everything we have been able to experience together. But there is a lot of uncertainty in my life. There are things I want to work through, and I think it will be better to just be friends. I really want to be able to maintain a friendship with you, though, and I don't want this to be the end of that. I'm sorry I've been distant. It's just been a really hard season for me. I really care about you, Rob."

Unable to stop an onslaught of tears, I replied, "I really care about you, too, Kelsey. School's been much tougher without your presence in my life, but I understand and deeply appreciate you sharing this, no matter how hard it was to say. I still very much want to be your friend and simply want what's best for you."

Embracing each other for a hug and further stream of tears, we said our final goodbyes, and I slipped out to the parking lot to find my way back to my temporary home. As I drove away, bathed with the grief and sadness of what would never be, I still felt the little child in me smile—for he knew that this grief, this loss, was not a sign of inadequacy or a mistake, but a sign that he had fully opened to the invitation of love.

The rest of my AIM rotation proved challenging. Despite my lovely B&B and the ability to use a local YMCA, I found myself stuck in the pains of a stinging loneliness, away from family, peers, and unexpectedly, romantic love. It is in these precise moments of grief, loneliness, and loss when an armor of clinical distance and busyness starts to look quite appealing. With its glistening sheen and promises of protection, armor has an allure that captures the minds of many, tricking them to think that there is a war in the external world, simply because there is a fire burning on the inside.

Cynical healthcare providers often walk the wards whispering about the wonders of this armor and how it has allowed them to get this far. At first glance, it would be easy to hypothesize that emotional armor protects from and counters the pain or death we see in the hospital setting. While there is no denying the extensive suffering we will bear witness to within the healthcare field, my theory about how the armor really develops involves more than just the suffering we see with patients.

Healthcare students and workers are not just technicians. They are humans with lives outside of the hospital walls. While this acknowledgment of humanity outside the profession might seem obvious, we as a society seem to stop there and forgo an exploration of the story going on inside that life. While most believe that life outside of work should not impact professional endeavors, no matter the profession, we have a massive disagreement about the bounds and methods for achieving this end.

Some people turn to armor in an attempt to shield themselves from painful emotions. Some people turn to anger and hostility, and outwardly project the negative emotions they feel onto coworkers so that they don't actually have to experience the emotions themselves. Still others direct aggression inward and crumble into a dark depression, despite continuing to function in the world as a hollow core.

While the hospital environment may be the "professional incubator" that promotes the building up of this armor, the real reasons so many wear it stem from hurt and pain at home. As our ability to handle the emotional pain, stress, and hurt away from the healthcare setting boils over, we can feel trapped with no other choice but to wear armor at work so that we can keep on performing our jobs.

In the first few weeks wearing armor, you can easily feel its weight, and you remember to take it off before the ride home. But as the body hardens and the weight of the armor becomes habituated to the human beneath, the armor finds its way outside of the hospital and into the place you call home. While there will be moments when you notice the armor again and remove its weight so that it can stay in the hospital, eventually the armor is entirely forgotten and becomes enmeshed with the soul it once sought to protect.

Even though the end of my relationship with Kelsey left me rediscovering isolation, I knew I did not want the armor. I knew love still needed to flow in. Unsure exactly how I could wear and bear my grief, I reflected on the wisdom of a dear friend from the UVA School of Nursing.

Before I returned to medical school, during my inner awakening and growth into more dedicated mindfulness practices, I joined a weekly morning meditation with accomplished nurse Jonathan Bartels. Because of its 6 a.m. start time, the meditation was lightly attended. But as I grew with that small group of regulars, I learned more about Jonathan and his efforts in our larger hospital system. During his time as an ER nurse, Jonathan began a simple act of reflection known as "The Pause." After the unfortunate death of a patient in the ER, Jonathan led the participating healthcare workers through a moment of silence and reflection on the life that was lost and the efforts of those who had attempted to save it. Removed of politics and religion, gender and titles, "The Pause" allowed healthcare workers to take off the armor—to feel and to be human once again. Giving space for emotion, giving space for that which makes us most alive, "The Pause" created a space for a reclamation of the humanity the armor sought so strongly to keep locked away inside.

You see, the hurt I experienced with the end of a relationship did not need to be a catalyst to an armor-wearing way of life. Grief could be felt, love could be shared, and I would be none the weaker when I put on my scrubs again.

≈ 30 ≈

They Don't Publish the Good News

Emergency Medicine, Internal Medicine—Hospital
October 2015

The weeks following the end of my relationship with Kelsey passed slowly, but with each reflective moment came greater and greater self-love. After the completion of my AIM rotation, I transitioned to a six-week, hospital-based Internal Medicine clinical rotation, my first real opportunity to showcase my growing medical knowledge and my overflowing human heart.

After the director of the hospital medicine rotation opened the discussion, he made way for our college dean to make an announcement. While our dean was one of the most joyful and caring people in our entire school—and the person instrumental to my earlier healing and continued progression through training—her presence there was entirely unexpected. Deans do not speak at rotation orientations.

Our dean openly sobbed through the painful details of the previous day. While driving back to Charlottesville to be present for the first day of our clinical rotation, my friend and classmate Juliana Porter had been killed in a car accident. She was dead before anyone could seek to save her life.

With some of her closest friends and classmates present in the room, the collective grief after hearing this news was almost too much to bear.

I thought I was done with losing, God. What the fuck are you up to now?

After I left the room in unbearable grief, I eventually found my way to my locker near the renovated anatomy lab. With my stained white coat still calling my shoulders home, I slumped to the floor and began to cry. Without concern for my appearance, for what anyone would think, I simply wanted to grieve the loss of my dear friend.

Over the span of a month, I had lost an emerging relationship, spent much of my time outside of school alone and away from loved ones, and now had just lost my first friend in my new medical school class. Thrown back into the previous years of repeated loss, I struggled to see the point of such unexpected and devastating blows; I struggled to see any reason to return to school at all.

Stuck in a maze of relentless mental chasms, I realized I needed some grounding to process Juliana's death. I needed to attend a meditation. Within minutes of joining a simple nursing school meditation, I felt the immediate sense of communal grieving. While I understood the immense healing potential of these meditation groups, I never expected to find such deep connection in the middle of such tremendous loss.

This particular meditation group was led by a gentle soul, Michael Swanberg, whose voice and compassion could lead you away from ruminative destruction in mere minutes. Unaware of my despair, Michael had prepared a special message and poem for the sitting. The poem was entitled "The Good News" by Thich Nhat Hanh.

> *They don't publish*
> *the good news.*
> *The good news is published*
> *by us.*
> *We have a special edition every moment,*
> *and we need you to read it.*
> *The good news is that you are alive,*
> *and the linden tree is still there,*
> *standing firm in the harsh Winter.*
> *The good news is that you have wonderful eyes*
> *to touch the blue sky.*
> *The good news is that your child is there before you,*
> *and your arms are available:*
> *hugging is possible.*
> *They only print what is wrong.*
> *Look at each of our special editions.*
> *We always offer the things that are not wrong.*
> *We want you to benefit from them*
> *and help protect them.*
> *The dandelion is there by the sidewalk,*
> *smiling its wondrous smile,*
> *singing the song of eternity.*
> *Listen! You have ears that can hear it.*
> *Bow your head.*
> *Listen to it.*

> *Leave behind the world of sorrow*
> *and preoccupation*
> *and get free.*
> *The latest good news*
> *is that you can do it.*

After Michael finished reading this poem, I could hardly bear the love rising up in my soul. Just like the tense moments I had spent in the operating room with a frustrated surgeon, just like the uncertain minutes I had spent engaged with positive psychology research subjects in thoughtful reflection, just like the timeless hours I had spent in unceremonious personal reflection, life continued to create unexplainable moments of healing potential. Without conscious intention or understanding, I was brought into intimate contact with other human beings serving as living conduits for healing and spiritual connection.

While we easily recognize the healing acts of doctors, nurses, therapists, and surgeons, we struggle mightily to see the mysterious but miraculous healing of romantic partners, children, and strangers alike. Until you consciously discover the joyful effect that a simple smile can have on an individual you previously didn't know, you may never fully believe in your innate power to love, to connect, and to heal. For these acts of unconscious healing to manifest, however, takes courage and faith on all sides. We must believe and recognize that the love and work we put into the world can positively affect those we may never actually see, while also recognizing that in order to receive such acts of unintended love we must be open and receptive to what doesn't seem possible.

Before I had experienced this phenomenon of unintended healing over and over again, I had no theory, no conscious awareness of its existence. After these miracles, these moments of incredible human connection, however, I could not unsee what had been there all along.

At the end of the meditation, I asked Michael if I could keep the poem. He handed it to me as if he had always known he would never take it home, and it made its way onto my desk and into my heart where it could never fade away.

Part III

Wearing a New White Coat

≈ 31 ≈

The Shift

Internal Medicine—Hospital
October 2015

I can't tell you when I came back to my internal medicine clerkship, but eventually I had no other choice. I may have returned the day after the meditation or the next week altogether. When I finally did come back, however, I could barely recognize the soul beneath my student white coat.

Throughout my third-year rotations, I had been "traditionally obedient." I showed up when I was supposed to, did my work and then some, and followed the rules of the system. While I continued to explore integrative and functional medicine outside of classwork, reading books, watching video lectures, and listening to podcasts, I had not let this knowledge seep out into my third-year efforts. Surgery was simply survival with little place even in the clinical setting for anything other than "let's cut something out." Pediatrics and obstetrics were also positively demanding, and I made sure to excel within the expectations placed upon me, but my integrative side was not on significant display. My AIM rotation was my first potential opportunity to showcase my lifestyle medicine approach, but the preceptor and the timing were just not right. Despite my yearning to engage my patients in discussions of lifestyle medicine and dietary treatments, I found myself scared of judgment, scrutiny, and misunderstanding. I understood the privilege of my position at a top medical school, and I knew very well the expectant hierarchy of students, residents, fellows, and attending physicians. Third-year medical students don't just go around telling patients what they should do. But this, my friends, was all about to change.

As I sat in my kitchen one night after listening to a lecture about autoimmunity and its connection to gut health and the gut microbiome, I realized it was time to walk my own way. Actively grieving the tragic loss of a dear friend with my own near-death experience and its suicidal premonitions still close in the rearview mirror, I finally saw through the veil of death and the shroud of fear we as a society placed over the unspoken taboo. Many people often say that they do not fear death, that they choose to live every day like it is their last, but frankly there is nothing poetic about this way of living, and when someone reaches the transition in life that would make this mantra more apropos, they are almost universally unable to live the way the saying suggests.

What I began to feel at my simple kitchen table was not a desire to be reckless, but an awakening of courage in the face of fear—the fear of rejection, the fear of failure, the fear of inadequacy, and yes still, the fear of death. I was not interested in living every day like it would be my last; I was much too cautious for that type of extreme outlook. *But when truly would I ever get the moment again as a student to impact the lives of the patients I was currently seeing?* When would I ever be able to learn from patients and physicians in such diverse circumstances? What would happen if the demands of the present moment and the patient's needs were different from the expectations that directly impacted my clinical grades? What would the attending doctors say in my clerkship reviews if I ended up being just like the hundreds of students that came before me?

What was holding me back from fully being me?

As if I had been catapulted back in time to the morning following my out-of-body experience in early 2013, the way forward was both as clear and as unexpected as before. The way forward required a new courage, a new engagement, a stepping out of fear altogether. Life was too short to not walk my own way.

∞ 32 ∞

The Singer

Acute Cardiac Service—Internal Medicine
November 2015

After my spiritual and mental shift during the hospital-based internal medicine rotation, I moved to the acute cardiac service (ACS), a demanding hospital unit that was led by several different cardiologists who cared for patients with acute heart conditions. While the patients were not sick enough to be in the cardiac intensive care unit, the ACS unit was home to some of the more chronically and acutely ill who suffered from diseases of the heart valves and blood vessels as well as irregular heart rhythms. The ACS rotation and its work demands were closer to my surgery rotation than anything else I had done before, but I was more than ready for the task. While the requirement to present patients to the larger medical team during our collective rounds was not new, this process was particularly nerve-racking and moved me to voraciously review cardiac physiology, pathology, and the many drugs I would encounter along the way.

Days into the service, I took over care for an obese man in his late fifties who had severe aortic stenosis, or a narrowing of the heart valve that released oxygenated blood from the heart to the rest of the body. Individuals who developed severe narrowing of this valve were susceptible to decreased blood flow out of the heart and to the rest of the body, including the brain. In addition, individuals commonly developed abnormal blood pressure and struggled to deliver enough blood and oxygen to peripheral tissues. Because of the abnormal blood flow mechanics, patients with aortic stenosis were at risk for big changes in blood volume and could, over time, develop heart failure as the heart fought to pump blood through the narrowed exit. The prognosis was not good, and this patient's condition was quite severe.

Early on in my initial interviews with him, I recognized that he was a relatively quiet soul. From southwestern Virginia, he also had a thick Southern accent. Between the two it would be easily to judge him as simply aloof and uninterested in his health. Since he spoke little with the treatment team, I could sense that my superiors were not particularly interested in spending a great deal of time rounding on his case.

One afternoon after rounds, I decided to go to his room to see if I could engage with him a little more. As I stepped into his room at the end of the hall, I found him slowly pacing and looking out of the windows around his room. After he acknowledged my presence, I walked inside and started up a conversation.

The gentleman was a devout Christian and had built his own small altar and church in his backyard. He was happy to show off pictures of his home for song and prayer, beaming like I had never seen before. After he shared stories about its construction and what they had done in the space, he started to talk about his passion for singing. Both humble and proud, he told me how he had even recorded some CDs of various Christian songs. Right on cue, his girlfriend came into the room and joined in the conversation. I discovered rather quickly through her that his singing talents were far greater than he was letting on. Unable to hide from his girlfriend's love and admiration, he shared one of his CDs with me so I could take it home and listen to his voice. Sticking the CD in my white coat, I made a mental note to take it out once the day was over. After nearly 45 minutes in his presence, I reported back to my supervising resident for afternoon check-ins and my final duties before the close of the day.

The following morning as I prepared to present my patient to the treatment team, I realized the CD was still in my pocket; I had forgotten to take it home. After I shared the most pertinent updates to the rest of our medical team waiting outside his room, we stepped inside so the attending physician could do his ceremonious hello and physical exam.

When I looked at my patient's face, I could sense that he was in a brighter, more vibrant mood. While he remained fairly quiet, I could tell that everyone in the room felt more at ease with his positive demeanor. Recognizing this vibrancy, the attending doctor asked how he was doing and why he was feeling better. Without saying anything, the patient simply turned in my direction and pointed straight at me. As I had already switched from "presentation mode" into "curious onlooking student mode," I was left a bit flat-footed as everyone now stared at me.

What in the world did the patient mean with his gesture?

"I feel like I am ready to go home now, if that is okay with you?" the patient asked.

Since his valvular condition did not appear operable, the cardiothoracic surgeons had recommended continued medical management in the outpatient setting. Now that the patient had fully voiced his desires, the medical plan was solidified. He would go back home to the things he loved.

After we left the room and completed the remainder of rounds, I helped the resident prepare the discharge summary paperwork. With these duties completed, I went back to the patient's room for our final goodbyes. Before I could even say a word, I was wrapped in a giant hug as tears streamed down his face. With those tears still visible, we sat down together to share in a final prayer. It was arguably the most touching moment of my third year, a year filled with tremendous joy but also, great, great sadness. As I left the room, I touched my hand inside my pocket to make sure the CD was still there. No matter where this man's life would take him next, he could never leave my soul.

After the final chapter of my ACS rotation was written, I packed up my things to travel to Staunton, Virginia, and my next rotation in family medicine with nationally renowned physician Dr. Robert Marsh.

With CD in hand, I stepped into my RAV4 to hear what my patient's heart sought to share with the world.

Taken aback almost immediately by the music, I was transfixed by both the vocals and the musical attunement he had produced to go with his voice. Between well-known Christian songs such as "I Can Only Imagine" and "How Great Is Our God" and others I had never heard before, I was left joyfully wordless and with an unexpected peace despite my lonely drive to another place away from home.

Over my four-week family medicine rotation, I listened to his CD during every drive from my temporary home in Staunton to the medical clinic in Raphine and back to my apartment in Charlottesville. While my hours were long and there were few minutes to spare anywhere in between, I found respite in the faithful joy that was my patient's music.

After I finished my family medicine rotation in mid-December, I returned to Charlottesville to enjoy a brief holiday. Still consumed by my patient's music, I traveled to the hospital one day to find his contact number in our electronic medical record system so that I could see how he had been doing since his discharge and share my deep appreciation for his music.

As I searched his medical record, I found a note from a phone conversation dated after his discharge from the hospital. In it, I saw in just a few lines that the patient's girlfriend had recently called to say he had passed away in his sleep on December 5, 2015. Stunned, I started to cry knowing that I would never have the chance to tell him how much his music and his presence had positively impacted my life. Crushed yet again by loss, I paused to reflect. Bathed in the serenity of the present moment, I heard his lyrical voice whisper softly in my ear, "You brought me the peace, Rob, that I needed so I could finally go."

33

Incubation

Family Medicine
Staunton, Virginia
November–December 2015

Even before my third-year clinical rotations, I had felt my passions in medicine were best suited for the field of family and integrative medicine. Because I wanted to care for patients across the spectrum of life, with no topic or body system off-limits, family medicine seemed like the most reasonable specialty for my broad-reaching efforts.

For my third-year clinical rotation in family medicine, I asked to work with Dr. Robert Marsh, a physician in Middlebrook, Virginia, who was well known for his teaching acumen and down-to-earth nature. While his practice and the rotation demanded much of medical students, I was looking for the greatest test my mind could handle at this stage of my clinical development.

Although whole books could be written about Dr. Marsh, two things stood out to me about this unique individual. First of all, he lived as if he possessed twenty-eight hours in his working day. Between rounds on his patients at the local hospital to home visits with those unable to make it to his clinic, he did everything except possibly sleep. The second and perhaps most admirable attribute about Dr. Marsh was his remarkable openness to students and their personal explorations.

The hierarchy within medicine continually creates distance between those who are "learned" and those who are "learning" with the learned seemingly not allowed or unable to pick up anything new from those that are learning. The learned vs. learning paradigm is an odd dynamic perpetuated across nearly every academic medical institution often in hidden and insidious forms. On my family medicine rotation with Dr. Marsh, however, I would encounter no residents, no fellows, and no vertical distance between anyone. I was an equal blessed to work with a collaborative team so that we could help our patients in need.

On my first day of the rotation, I got oriented to their electronic medical record system with the help of two of his supporting scribes. They gave me a laptop computer and told me to see a certain number of patients on the master list for the day. With no rope or leash, I set out into each room alone, ready to collect the patient's history and share my personal knowledge without fear of judgment from any supervisor. After each patient, I came out of the exam room and worked on my note while I waited for Dr. Marsh so that I could present my findings, assessment, and plan. This clinical routine continued for several hours as Dr. Marsh performed the same pattern with the two scribes. By the end of the first day, I had several patient charts to finalize and needed to take my computer home in order to finish my notes before another early start at the hospital the next day. While I objectively faced a future of similar days and sleep-deprived nights with little time for myself in between, I strangely felt remarkably freed to fully be me.

As I shared the depths of our patients' stories with Dr. Marsh, I felt the presence of a supervising doctor who not only listened to everything I shared, but affirmed my plans and suggestions for many lifestyle-based therapies. While I recognized Dr. Marsh supported and affirmed essentially all of the medical students who passed through his clinic, I knew I was particularly driven, overflowing with ideas for lifestyle and naturopathic therapies. Despite not being well-versed in some of the things I recommended, he saw that my suggestions were valid and compassionate and so supported me in everything I pursued with curious inquiry.

While I completed my duties with his two clinics in Raphine and Middlebrook as well as the main hospital in Fishersville, I commuted back and forth between all of these locations from a new temporary home in Staunton where I stayed in a beautiful, small house just above the railroad tracks that coursed their way through the center of town. From the top of the hill on which the house sat, I could take in the fullness of the night sky above. I walked a regular loop from the hilltop across town to a local park called Gypsy Hill. While I had been to Gypsy Hill in the summer of 2013 during my work as a YMCA camp counselor, the park was now entirely transformed for the winter holidays into a massive display of lights and joyful cheer. Between the hundreds of reindeer with their flashing LEDs and the waves of decorative lighting displays constructed by local businesses, Gypsy Hill was a glowing wonder for all to share and appreciate. While my mornings and days were filled with medical duties, my evening walks through the lights of Gypsy Hill grounded me into the present, the inescapable joy God had left for me.

Two months had passed since the end of my relationship with Kelsey. With Juliana's death and the insane bustle of school, I had had no space to explore a new relationship. Anchored now with the pulse of Staunton, the challenges of loneliness revved up in my heart.

How could it be this hard to find someone to share in a sacred human connection?

With no one other than God around to listen, I asked for some help, some guidance, some solace in this new storm. I had spent nearly three years in a personal incubator to grow my self-awareness and my capacity to love. *Wasn't it time I found someone with whom I could share in this collective human experience?*

With whispers whistling through the wintery night, the silence of Nature, the echoes of Spirit were clear.

Patience, young Soul, the incubator is still your home.

Toward the end of my family medicine rotation with Dr. Marsh, I made a surprise trip to nearby Yogaville in order to visit my friends from the Viniyoga training program I had started earlier that summer. While I could not join the group for its second intensive program because of my medical school obligations, I wanted to visit and see the faces and hearts that had touched me so dearly a few months before.

After I made my way into the Yogaville complex, I slipped into the main teaching hall and quietly climbed the stairs. As I snuck into the back of the room while class carried onward, my teacher Gary Kraftsow noticed my presence and made a joyous statement to the group. I stayed for some time with the group as part of an unexpected reunion of connection and love and even walked some of the trails to experience the energy of this sacred space.

My inner fire, which had grown so dim amid the challenges of medical school, the loss of a relationship, and the loss of a dear friend, was renewed by my connections with the Earth and with other humans who simply wanted the same. During these moments of renewal and concomitant surrender, my whole being knew without words that my cup was full again, ready to be shared, and that indeed, the incubator—as it had been for my first weeks of life within this miraculous world—could still be a home for a heart that just wanted to love.

34

The Unknown

Neurology and Psychiatry
December 2015–March 2016

At Yogaville, I reconnected with a yoga teacher from Davidson named Sam and another yoga teacher and nurse from Pittsburgh named Amy. Amy and I had spent some time together during the first training session, connected by our medical backgrounds and other shared interests. I found her personal spiritual practice and the ways in which she blended her work in nursing and passions for yoga rather fascinating. While I struggled to continually make meaning from the labors of medicine and integrate my compassionate nature and spiritual practices into my work as a healer, Amy was a shining light to awaken what I only unconsciously knew to be there.

After our reunion in Yogaville, Amy and I stayed connected and talked on the phone between our individually busy schedules. Given the physical distance between us and our significant difference in age, our relationship only held the promise of supportive friendship. However, the emotional and spiritual side of me kept asking, "What if?"

As our emotional and spiritual bond deepened, I felt the strong desire to at least spend more time with her in person so I could see her work as a yoga teacher.

During the last few days of my holiday break, I traveled up to Pittsburgh to stay with Amy. Over the course of several days, we attended multiple yoga classes, hiked, cooked, and explored a new spiritual world. It was blissful and raw as we both sought to erase the societal and practical realities that stood in the way of a deeper relationship.

After I returned to Charlottesville to start my next rotation in neurology, however, the reality and challenges for our relationship became clearer and clearer by the day. With my demanding schedule and her obligations at home, time to connect on the phone was hard to come by, and we simply could not meet each other's needs. In mid-February, Amy came to visit for Valentine's Day. While we shared in a few joyful experiences together, we realized we needed to be spiritually supportive friends and that was all our relationship could ever be.

The next week I started on the final rotation of my third year—psychiatry. While my mind was set to pursue a career in family medicine, my heart responded to the conflicted world of psychiatry. I was quite disillusioned with the modern practice of psychiatry, a profession dominated by pharmaceuticals instead of psychological support, and worried what a training residency would entail for someone with my perspective and heart. In addition, the field of psychiatry struggled to reconcile the unified body-mind, and I did not see an easy way to bring my knowledge of physiology, biochemistry, and nutrition into a domain punishingly focused on the brain.

My psychiatry rotation was designed to provide me with inpatient experience, where I would work with the acute stabilization unit of the hospital as well as the consulting service that cared for the hospitalized patients with psychiatric concerns outside of their primary medical complaints.

With the arrival of my final third-year rotation, I had to confront the odd reality of my third-year grades. While the preclinical years of medical school followed a pass-fail structure, the third-year rotations reverted back to standardized letter grades. Outside of family medicine, each individual rotation—surgery, pediatrics, obstetrics/gynecology, internal medicine, and neurology—involved a combination of graded assignments, personal evaluations, clinical examinations, and a larger cumulative multiple-choice test. In order to receive an A for the rotation, I needed to get great personal evaluations, perform well on clinical assignments, and score highly on the final multiple-choice exam. My collective academic work had not yet resulted in the necessary ingredients to receive an A. Remarkably, in all of the clerkships thus far, I had managed to pull a B+. With consistent B's on almost all cumulative multiple-choice exams, passing grades on clinical assessments, and above average personal evaluations, I was the quintessential B+ student. On my internal medicine rotation, I somehow managed to get an 89.4%—something I thought only happened in students' nightmares. Alas, the computer did not lie: An 89.4% B+ was what I had.

What would it finally take to get an A?

I started the psychiatric rotation with a two-week period on the inpatient acute stabilization unit. As part of the rotation, I was paired with another medical student as well as two second-year psychiatry residents. Together, the four of us worked to care for half of the patients on the unit while another equivalent team took care of the others.

During the first day of the rotation, as we got oriented with rounding procedures and student expectations, I got my team assignment and met some of the psychiatry residents including those directing my team. Globally, the psychiatry residents were the happiest and most genuine residents I had worked with to date. Eager to teach, they did not see medical students as simply pawns to cover the work they were employed to do. I felt accepted and at home with this group.

On my particular team, I was partnered with a quiet and beautiful psychiatry resident named Selene. Selene looked like she could have been a model instead of a doctor, but here she was as a psychiatry resident. Throughout the first few days, I came to better understand Selene's quiet and exacting nature. She was precise and had little tolerance for unnecessary action. During rounds she also looked as if she were on the verge of constantly falling asleep. Because of her apparent fatigue and quietness, she seemed confused about my ideas and actions on the inpatient unit. As I operated somewhere between a "gunning" high-achieving student and someone who made his own rules, it was no wonder I was an enigma for her. I always got my work done and cared for my patients at the highest level, though, so she recognized my work ethic and had few questions for me as we cared for our patients.

Each day on the unit with Selene only made me more curious about her. She was the most beautiful and mysterious woman I had ever met, and I desperately wanted to understand the world behind her often closed eyes.

Her complexion hinted at a diverse background, perhaps African American, Indian, or something in Southeast Asia. Her face was narrow and carved to perfection. Her eyebrows seemed like they were drawn on, and her lips were soft, but tense with thought. Her walk was more like angelic floating, her only solution to the workload dragging resident physicians into depressive oblivion. Beyond tired, she hid both her beauty and pain behind straightened dark hair. There was no mistaking it. She wore what my grandfather called "the sign."

LOVE ME.

I pictured a world where I could have a conversation with her outside of the realm of medicine, where I could unravel the mystery behind how she had ended up here, where I could finally connect with someone to whom I clearly gravitated so strongly.

As I jumped out of this reverie, I berated myself for following such a ridiculous fantasy. She was a resident, and I was a medical student. I knew nothing about her, and such thoughts were likely just a product of my failing efforts to find someone with whom I could spiritually and physically connect in this bizarre world.

But then again, who doesn't imagine themselves with the most beautiful and mysterious person they have ever met?

35

Inertia

*Physical Medicine and Rehabilitation,
Developmental Pediatrics
March 2016*

With the completion of my third-year rotations, I had reached the promised land, the beckoning oasis of fourth year. While the third year of school was packed to the gills with clinical duties in which I had no say, fourth-year students could select less burdensome elective rotations to broaden their medical school experience beyond the core specialty fields. Between the more humane hours and my growing clinical acumen, fourth year brought a deepening sense of control to my intense academic life. Over the course of two weeks, I spent time with several different residents and fellows as part of a rotation in physical medicine and rehabilitation. Focusing on sports medicine, I followed the runners and athletes clinic led by Dr. Robert Wilder and observed unique procedures designed to alleviate pain and spasticity in suffering patients. After that, I took part in a developmental pediatrics rotation where I worked with physicians focused on the early development of children. Challenged by a spectrum of developmental, motor, and speech disorders, I witnessed massive variations and capacities in children of seemingly the same age.

During one aspect of the developmental pediatric rotation, I worked with one of the pediatric neurologists with whom I had connected during my third-year neurology rotation. We saw children in the hospital suffering from various neurologic conditions. In many cases, these patients experienced intractable seizures and were often on cocktails of medications to minimize the frequency and severity of those episodes. During my first week, we cared for a patient who continued to have breakthrough seizures on no fewer than five medications. After sitting down with the mother and realizing I didn't know of any options to give her, I resolved to explore all possible avenues to help her son.

At this point, I had read extensively about the potential for a specialized diet known as a ketogenic diet to address a number of neurologic conditions—including epilepsy and refractory seizures in children. While I knew implementing such a diet would be incredibly challenging given the patient's social and family situation, the dietary concept was at least one nontoxic approach we could explore to try to alleviate the patient's continued seizures. As I dug further, I explored more investigational therapies for various seizure conditions. Somewhere along the way, I stumbled across the potential for cannabidiol or CBD—a cannabinoid extracted from cannabis—to treat refractory seizures. While CBD would explode into the mainstream in 2019, the landscape and awareness of CBD in early 2016 were decidedly quiet. I discovered a company called GW Pharmaceuticals that was actively implementing a Phase III study for a CBD drug to treat a couple of rare, treatment-resistant epilepsy syndromes. The drug did not yet have a name and was simply referred to by a series of numbers and letters. While we weren't looking at an FDA-approved CBD drug yet, the possibilities for cannabis and specifically CBD were encouraging. For this particular patient with few treatment options, dietary changes and CBD seemed to offer unexpected hope.

Now, for a normal or even a slightly odd medical student to take these researched ideas any further than their own mind would be a significant deviation from clinical expectations. Medical education, as I've outlined before, is based on the learned and the learning, and within these hierarchical structures exist the frameworks of the "acceptable known" and the "unacceptable unknown." Supervising doctors and resident physicians who have worked with hundreds of medical students know what to expect and what medical students will share. Medical students will know everything about the patient and usually have a solid working knowledge of the patient's condition as chronicled from the popular medical encyclopedia UpToDate. Medical students will assess the obvious and make plans that are logical and within accepted norms. While medical students will certainly stray from the expected domain on many occasions, their forays into the wilderness are usually out of ignorance or naivety and not because of an intentional effort.

I, however, was not a normal or even a slightly odd medical student.

In fact, in the final weeks of my previous psychiatry rotation during a larger educational meeting known as grand rounds, I had chosen to speak up during a discussion between supervising doctors that I found far too certain for my liking. In the discussion, the supervising doctors described a case of an individual with complex psychological suffering. Because of certain observed characteristics of the patient, the doctors had decided that certain treatment modalities—all nonpharmacological I might add—were not possible. It is one thing to argue that a certain drug would be unlikely to provide a certain patient benefit based on its understood mechanism of action; it is another thing entirely to demonstrably say that certain active, nonpharmacological therapies will not work because other people seemingly similar to this patient did not benefit.

And so I spoke up. In a room full of superiors where the small white coats are supposed to just show up and shut up.

"I don't agree with what you have said. I don't see why she couldn't find benefit in some of the treatments you say are not possible."

That was just who I am.

Fuck the hierarchy. The hierarchy is dead.

So, back in the present day, as I met with the supervising doctor during rounds, I brought my research findings to the table. Given the supervising doctor's understanding of my broader interests and passions within medicine, my suggestions did not fall completely on deaf ears, but the invariable way forward did not involve an exploration of CBD or a ketogenic diet.

This was the world I lived in throughout medical school—I was a helpless bystander bulldozed by a medical system with more inertia than an eighteen-wheeler. What could be more demoralizing than knowing we could be doing more to relieve a patient's suffering, but being handcuffed by a medical system that limits what is acceptable and thus possible. At many points along my medical school journey, I struggled to see the point of sharing my unique ideas.

Would I just feel disappointed over and over again about what would never be explored? Would I just feel rejected with every idea shot down?

Was all this caring worth it?

As my mind battled my heart, my soul spoke out with the distilled wisdom my entire being needed to hear.

The care you desire need not manifest to prove you cared for it at all.

36

The Test to Nowhere

Philadelphia
April 2016

With my completion of the third-year rotations, I was eligible to take the next set of board exams as part of my medical training. Divided into two portions known as the Step 2 CK, or Clinical Knowledge, and Step 2 CS, or Clinical Skills, the board exams were designed to assess a student's knowledge and skills gleaned from the clinical years. I didn't necessarily need to take these exams until much later in my fourth year of school, but the material assessed on the Step 2 CK portion would only get foggier the further I moved from my third-year clinical experience.

As with my Step 1 exam, my Step 2 prep started well before my formal decision to take the test. To prepare for the CK portion, I answered questions from preparatory question banks for several months in order to familiarize myself with the types of questions I would encounter during the exam itself. Like Step 1, Step 2 CK would present me with clinical scenarios and questions that would conflict greatly with my personal views, forcing me to choose their "correct" answer in lieu of my own beliefs and perceptions of what I felt would be medically appropriate. Prepared to jump again into the land of internal conflict, it took me arguably more energy to mentally prepare for the dissonance of the test than to review the material covered in the questions themselves.

While Step 2 CK was structured similarly to the multiple-choice format of Step 1, Step 2 CS was an entirely different test. Step 2 CS was designed to assess an individual's clinical skills as a physician. The test required me to participate in various clinical scenarios where I would interview a standardized or "acting" patient, collect a history, and perform a physical exam. Following the history and exam, I would provide this patient with a general assessment and tentative diagnostic plan and then leave the room to articulate these thoughts in an electronic note.

While my description of Step 2 CS may make it sound like a reasonable assessment of a medical student's clinical skills, the test is sadly anything but. Let's pause for a second and think about what a clinical assessment for medical students should entail. I propose these key competencies as a starting place: 1. Can the student demonstrate competency in communication with the patient beyond just a grasp of the English language and medical jargon? 2. Can the student empathize and connect with the patient beyond the medical complaint for which they are being evaluated? 3. Can the student demonstrate compassionate listening using teach/read-back techniques with the patient? 4. Can the student adequately articulate their understanding of the patient's concerns without the use of medical jargon? 5. Can the student provide a therapeutic plan that is in line with the patient's values and personal desires and not just the "gold standard" for the symptoms or complaint? 6. Can the student engage in a thorough discussion regarding informed consent behind a specific treatment, explaining risks, benefits, alternatives, and expectations regarding the treatment? 7. Can the student engage in a discussion with a family regarding end-of-life care and decision-making for a loved one who is near death? My list of questions could go on and on, but I will stop here for the sake of this exploration.

Now as an individual—whether medical or non-medical—you may look at my clinical competency list and think, *well yes, I would like a physician who can adequately demonstrate all of these qualities and skills.* But although your expectations and desires for such a clinician is beyond reasonable, no medical student anywhere in the United States has to demonstrate *any* of these seven suggested competencies and skills on the Step 2 CS exam. Not one. The closest any of the actual Step 2 CS examination competencies gets to my suggested skills is number 1, where individuals must demonstrate competency in communication involving the English language only, without a specific requirement for successful articulation without the use of medical jargon.

The test has no requirement for real empathy; no requirement for deep listening using teach-back techniques to confirm a student's understanding; no requirement to be an articulate teacher, informing the patient about their condition or situation in terms they can understand; no requirement for developing a personalized plan in line with a patient's interests that may include a desire to not pursue drugs, surgery, or expensive therapies; no requirement to demonstrate competency in obtaining full informed consent; and no requirement to engage in the difficult discussions around the end of life.

So what in the hell are we assessing with our doctors in training?

Let me give you a few more important details about this assessment. Step 2 CS involves twelve separate interviews. Twelve. The student has fifteen minutes to conduct the interview portion and ten minutes to articulate their interview and assessment in a list-based note. Many individuals who take the test find the ten minutes provided to think and write to be inadequate, so they keep the interview to around ten minutes. Ten.

I don't know about you, but why in the world would we assess communication and clinical skills via twelve fifteen-minute interviews and list-based notes rapidly constructed in under ten minutes?

What does any of this prove?

In my opinion, next to nothing.

As the test currently stands, a student can pass simply by acting like a robot, faking empathy, and performing very small portions of a simulated exam. Individuals can also pass this test writing list-based notes with poorly articulated thoughts and ideas because, well, you have ten minutes. A passing score on Step 2 CS proves absolutely nothing about a student's competency, and sadly, many entirely competent and compassionate doctors will fail this test because of its contrived and ridiculous construction.

To make this all the more ironic, when you go to the USMLE Step 2 CS testing website, under the FAQ section you will find the question "What evidence is there that the design of Step 2 CS is sound?" Their answer? A list of five study citations with the latest in 2013. The

USMLE can't even provide us with a basic description of the test's validity and simply throws out a list of studies to give us the impression that the test is evidence based as a clinically reliable assessment. For anyone who is curious, a wider internet search also demonstrates that I am not the only physician who wants to see significant reform to Step 2 CS or the elimination of it entirely.

If we actually decided to keep Step 2 CS around, what should the test look like?

If we start with the proposition that we are focused on the assessment of the skills I've just outlined, I could adequately assess these seven domains by observing students for around two hours as part of three to four different scenarios lasting twenty to forty minutes each. I would do away with rapid note creation as that does not support any of my competency questions. Zero. I would also say that for this particular test, I would not even be interested in the medical accuracy of a student's assessment and suggested plan since these factors can be assessed in a more effective manner on another test. I would simply want to understand the student's ability to communicate, to listen, to empathize, to construct a value-congruent plan, and to simply *be* with patients and their needs—not *any* patient with the same symptoms, but the patient in front of them at that very moment.

Our healthcare system can only be as good as our doctors, and our doctors can only be as good as the training they undertake. We do not need robots, technicians, and cynical zombies. We need competent, compassionate, and articulate individuals who listen first and speak second. We need empathizers and feelers. We need individuals not afraid of the difficult conversations. We need individuals who can honor the patient's wishes even if those are different from their own expectations. If we want physicians with these skills, we must value these skills enough to include them in their training. And if we want our physicians to maintain and share these skills, we must stop killing them slowly before they even leave "the womb" of the educational system.

Afterword

In early 2021, amid challenges in the implementation of a virtual Step 2 CS exam and the continued complaints from physicians about its expensive and ineffective construction, the National Board of Medical Examiners (NBME) permanently canceled Step 2 CS as I have described it to you. The NBME appear to have no intentions of implementing a replacement test.

37

Functional Medicine

Integrative Medicine Elective Rotation
Pittsburgh
May 2016

As I planned out my fourth year of elective education, I scoured the internet and medical schools across the country to find an "away" elective in integrative medicine. While UVA was a major academic and research hospital, the medical center did not have a formal integrative medicine department or any integrative medicine student electives. Although I was acquainted with some of the physicians at UVA involved in medical yoga and mindfulness, I knew I could not have a robust integrative medicine experience in Charlottesville, so the search was on.

After perusing several options in early January, I stumbled upon an integrative medicine elective rotation at the University of Pittsburgh Medical Center. The clinic was adjacent to the UPMC Shadyside Hospital and offered a four-week elective for all medical students. With the opportunity to stay with Amy during the rotation, the elective in Pittsburgh seemed like the perfect fit. But as with many of my previous efforts at "planned out" joy, my impressions of how things would go in January 2016 when I made these plans did not actually match reality when May came around.

While the exploration of our relationship ended shortly into the year, Amy and I were still on amicable terms, and she realized I could not afford a place to stay in Pittsburgh for the four weeks of the rotation. She made a place for me in a separate room of her house, and I arrived in early May ready for a new experience.

Just a few days into my stay, however, life with Amy was not going well. With tensions and poor communication abounding, the atmosphere was not of a resolving friendship ready to move forward.

"What are you eating? That seems a little odd," she mused as I sat over some cooked vegetables I had just prepared in her kitchen.

"Amy, I am just eating the food I normally eat. I am worried this is not going in a very constructive direction."

"I am just saying it's kind of odd."

"Okay, Amy."

The next day, it continued.

"Do you really want to be here?" she asked.

"I would really like to complete this rotation, but it is very stressful being in your house right now. I appreciate you letting me stay here, but I think it would be better for us if I tried to stay somewhere else."

"It would probably be easier to just stay here," she replied.

"I think it would be better for us both if I didn't."

I went outside and called up my previous medical school roommate Nick Hac, who was now working as a resident physician with UPMC. He was living with his fiancée, Rachel, remarkably close to the Shadyside

Hospital, so he suggested I stay with them to finish out the rotation.

Coming back inside, I shared my new plan with Amy.

"I am going to stay with my friends Nick and Rachel starting tomorrow. I will go to their place after my clinic day. I think we just need more time apart for things to heal."

Over the first week of the integrative medicine rotation, I met acupuncturists, chiropractors, massage therapists, myofascial body workers, and integrative medicine physicians. Inside of a rather old and odd clinical building with its rainbow of healers, I felt an opening of wonder as I witnessed patients receive the holistic care their hearts most desperately desired. While I could have certainly stayed in the presence of these various healers, my own heart longed for something more.

In the second week of my rotation, I met Dr. Karl Holtzer. Dr. Holtzer had been a longtime pediatrician, but had suffered numerous health challenges with his arm, which made practice as a traditional pediatrician essentially impossible. After a serendipitous journey into functional and lifestyle medicine, Dr. Holtzer now saw both adults and children who were looking for an integrative approach to their chronic health concerns. Within minutes of meeting Karl, I could sense an instant connection, a blast of joy shared between a curious medical student and a functional medicine practitioner who recognized the role of nutrition and lifestyle to address chronic disease.

Like a bucket ready to overflow, all of the articles, studies, videos, and trainings I had pursued outside of medical school now bubbled out into the real world for Karl and his patients. While he could have easily felt annoyed by my clinical intrusions, Karl embraced my enthusiasm and insights with open arms. Recognizing my clinical passions and wealth of knowledge, Karl was overjoyed to finally have someone with whom he could share his own clinical passions and endeavors. With a deepening acceptance, understanding, and love for our shared clinical interests, I was in heaven with Karl and never wanted to leave.

Over the course of those few weeks, I felt more like a clinician and less like a student than ever before. As I practiced in the scope and style I had always imagined for my future clinic, I finally felt the integration of my naturopathic approach and my expressions of mindful, compassionate living.

Oh, the dream, the dream.

Could it come true after all?

38

What You Don't See

Haiti
July 2016

As part of our family medicine rotations, my classmates and I were matched with various physicians across the state. While I spent my family medicine hours with Dr. Marsh in Middlebrook, my fellow classmate Liz spent time in Charlottesville with family physician Dr. Greg Gelburd. Liz knew about my interests in yoga, meditation, and pretty much everything outside of the box, so she immediately recognized that Greg and I needed to meet. She sent me Greg's contact information, and I used it to email him in early 2016, not really knowing what to expect. With Greg's reply just seventeen minutes later, I was off to the races to meet Greg and find out his visions for the world.

Like Dr. Marsh, Greg operated his clinic and his life by his own rules. His family medicine clinic was one of the last privately owned clinics, eschewing the possibility of a Sentara or UVA takeover. The clinic was home to several integrative-minded clinicians including Dr. Deidre Donovan as well as functional medicine practitioner Melanie Dorion, NP.

Within minutes of our first meeting for coffee, Greg's boisterousness and pure joy were quite apparent. While he could have been talking to everybody else in the room given the volume of his voice, Greg spoke to me with a youthful joy that never suggested he was almost sixty-five. As one of the first family physicians in Charlottesville to practice with a more holistic view, Greg incorporated homeopathy and spirituality into his work with patients and their families and crafted a personal style that engendered enduring trust and love.

Recognizing that spending time with Greg would be invaluable for my greater clinical education, I sought once again to create an elective experience to fit my unique interests. After a brief fight with the regulations of my academic system, I was finally approved to receive four weeks of credit as part of an elective rotation with Greg and his family medicine clinic.

During the first few weeks of our time together, Greg and I cared for patients within his clinic as well as for mothers and their newborn babies at one of the local nurseries. One morning before clinic, he notified me that we needed to do a home visit to see a mom who had just given birth to a baby boy. When we showed up at the house and I walked inside, there was none other than my friend Corey from the farmers market resting with her baby on the sofa.

After I got Greg up to speed on Corey's and my friendship, we proceeded to check on her new baby, Silas. Only in the world for just a few short days, Silas was just beginning his journey in the great unknown. As I listened to his fast-beating heart, I couldn't help but think about my miraculously "small world" and the never-ending spiral of human connection that God had planned for me.

In addition to the clinic hours, Greg planned for us to take a trip to Haiti to work as part of his foundation that medically and socially supported Haitians caring for other Haitians. Through education and empowerment and the sharing of medical supplies, Greg's vision was one of internal determination, where the Haitians themselves were invested in the process of communal care. Recognizing that millions of dollars had been poured into the country without an acknowledgment of what Haitians actually wanted and could sustain, Greg knew he needed to teach locals how to support themselves while he supplied them with a few things to do it along the way.

With our bags packed to the seams with supplies and medications, we flew to Haiti in the peak of summer. Once on the ground, we were picked up in a small truck that took us to the team house for the first night. Within minutes of the drive, I began to fully realize what kind of world I had just entered.

While I had traveled extensively with my family to various parts of the world, I had never been to a place like Haiti. My time in Haiti involved trips to both rural and urban settings, but the feeling of the country was the same no matter the location—of a place suffering with poverty beyond measure. Despite the immense poverty and a lack of infrastructure to provide even adequate sanitation, the Haitian people we met and the caretakers we trained were some of the most joyous people I had ever known. Carried by their faith and their community, this small group of humans sought to support their fellow Haitians no matter their limitations or practical means.

After an educational and spiritual retreat with the caretakers, we transitioned to host daily clinics for hundreds of local Haitians. In our bare-bones clinic, tasks were delegated to the caretakers and our small team. From check-in and water provision to the assessment of blood pressure and medication reconciliation, the clinic was organized and ready to serve. Alongside Greg and a physician from the Dominican Republic, I acted as the third primary "physician" to support the Haitian people. With Greg's reassurance and faith in my skills and the generosity of a team of translators, the three of us worked tirelessly to meet the physical and spiritual needs of our patients. While I had previously experienced the touching gratitude of patients and their families during my time as a medical student at UVA, nothing could have prepared me for what I experienced in Haiti.

Time and time again, patients asked if they could pray for my family and me, often bursting into tears of joy for the care we provided them. The raw emotion was overwhelming as the truth and depth of their intentions at prayer were undeniable. While Americans will commonly say, "I will pray for you," during times of challenge, for the Haitians this did not feel like such a hollow script; their hearts did the talking before their minds could even catch up. This Haitian community had next to nothing, and at the same time it had so much in spirit.

With one of my last patients of the day, I listened through a translator to a young woman's health challenges as she tearfully shared them. As the woman had recently received a foot massage from my friend Caitlin, who had set up an impromptu station for individuals to receive massages and some frankincense essential oil I had accidentally brought on the trip, she was in a more peaceful state than when she had arrived. As I continued to talk about how she could consider consuming different amounts of her available foods to improve her blood sugar, she nodded along and joyfully cried away at this seemingly most simple of suggestions.

"Yes, I can do that, Doctor. Bless you. God bless you."

Where in America had we lost our way?

Greg and I eventually returned to the United States in early August with empty bags but hearts filled with love. While it would have been easy for an onlooker to say that we were the ones that provided all of the healing, it was actually the patients we met and the community they called home that were the real healers of us all.

～ 39 ～

The Mother

Pediatric Gastroenterology
August 2016

After I returned from Haiti, I began a short rotation in pediatric gastroenterology, where I worked with specialists who treated kids with various gastrointestinal (GI) disorders. As I had already spent some time with these specialty pediatricians during my third-year pediatrics rotation, I was intrigued to focus intently on the health of the gut.

At this point in my clinical education, I reveled in the exploration of how the gut impacted our overall health. Throughout the 2010s, I witnessed a rapid evolution in our understanding of the gut microbiome—the vast network of "foreign" microorganisms that called our intestines home. As I sought to reconcile what was really behind the symptom categorizations such as irritable bowel syndrome (IBS) and gastroesophageal reflux disease (GERD) and elucidate the real roots of gut-based autoimmune conditions such as inflammatory bowel disease (IBD), I feverishly explored articles and podcasts that delved into the function of our intestinal barrier and how the disruption of the microbial ecosystem in the gut was associated with disease.

As part of the rotation, like my time with the pediatric neurologists, I saw hospitalized patients with various gut-related conditions. During one of my weeks in the hospital, I was paired with pediatric gastroenterologist Dr. Sean Moore. Dr. Moore was an accomplished doctor who actually spent the majority of his time in the research lab instead of the hospital or pediatric clinic. Since the primary physicians who usually covered the hospital service were out on vacation, we cared for a handful of children with serious GI conditions.

Early in our week together, we assumed the care of a teenage boy with severe ulcerative colitis. Ulcerative colitis (UC) is an autoimmune condition that affects the large intestine or colon. Categorized under the larger header of inflammatory bowel disease, individuals with UC suffer from severe inflammation of the colon that can lead to significant mucosal ulcerations and even strictures in the colon itself. Most patients with UC experience frequent, bloody bowel movements, as well as abdominal pain, and often become significantly malnourished because of poor dietary intake and malabsorption.

In the case of our teenage UC patient, things did not look good. He had suffered a waxing and waning disease course, but now was having a more significant flare-up. With his immune system markedly revved up, he experienced frequent bowel movements and became anemic given the systemic inflammation, nutritional deficits, and blood loss in his stool. Despite the gravity of his condition, his parents were steadfast in their hope for his recovery.

Early on during one of my conversations with his mother, whom I will call Marie, I learned a little more about the patient's life and his goals for the future. In addition to his UC, the patient had been diagnosed with narcolepsy, a rare neurological condition that affects the sleep-wake cycles of the body. While the exact causes of narcolepsy remain elusive, research suggests that at least some forms of narcolepsy are autoimmune in nature, whereby key structures necessary to maintain normal sleep-wake cycles are damaged by a malfunctioning immune system. While individuals with one autoimmune condition often develop other immune-mediated issues, I was shocked to see a young man with such a rare combination.

As we delved deeper into the patient's family dynamic, Marie's love and determination for her son became even more apparent. On seemingly every patient visit, Marie was right there alongside her son with several questions for me. While most physicians and medical students would have found Marie's questions and insistence annoying, I was amazed to finally find an advocate, a mother who wanted the best for her son. Marie sifted through the consideration of all therapeutic options in the context of their faith and values and showed her love for her son in every way possible.

As her son's health continued to decline, my heart ached over the lost time, the lost opportunity to have prevented this severe flare-up. Individuals with such severe UC that affects the body systemically almost universally require a surgery known as a colectomy to stop the incessant tide of inflammation. As part of the colectomy, a surgeon removes essentially all components of the colon and leaves the patient with a permanently altered digestive tract.

Now you might wonder, how in the world can anyone survive without a colon? While the complete answer to that question is rather complex, the simple version is that we can survive because the majority of essential digestion and nutrient absorption occurs in the small intestine, and so the large intestine becomes somewhat dispensable. Additionally, after the primary colectomy, many individuals go on to have a surgery to create a J-pouch that allows them to store and pass stool from the small intestine into the anus instead of into an ostomy bag. After this second surgical procedure, the portion of the small intestine used to make the J-pouch begins to resemble the large intestine in terms of its resident microbiome. While this change is likely adaptive for humans and improves overall survival following the removal of the large intestine, individuals can go on to develop acute and chronic infections of this special section of intestine. The way forward without a colon is neither straight nor easy, and I wanted to pursue any way possible to avoid this surgery for our patient.

As my discussions with Marie and her husband ranged from prognosis to treatment, I shared some of my interests in nutrition and lifestyle medicine. I told them that some individuals with IBD were able to control their condition using dietary approaches such as the Specific Carbohydrate Diet (SCD) or a nutrient-dense elimination diet known as the Autoimmune Protocol (AIP). While the potential for one of these dietary patterns as part of the healing process was undeniable, food adjustments alone in their son's dire circumstances would not save our patient's colon.

After what seemed like an eternity, we finally moved forward with a colectomy. The patient ultimately did very well in surgery and spent a few more days in the hospital to recover. Although he was still weak from malnutrition and the impact of the major surgery, the constant immune battle with his intestines was tempered.

You could easily look at the sequence of events with our patient and suggest that all my time with Marie to answer her questions, to hold space for her son, and to ignite a hope that we could avoid a colectomy simply put off the inevitable and denied the severity of her son's illness. But my time with Marie, bathed in a mother's warming presence, revealed instead that while medicine and surgery could solve the issue of the inflamed colon, only that most unexplainable act of human connection and love would ever allow him to heal.

⁓ 40 ⁓

The Red Paper Clip

Institute for Functional Medicine: AFMCP
Baltimore
September 2016

From September to October, I stayed busy with my self-constructed medical education. In early September, I drove to Baltimore to take part in a weeklong foundational training in functional medicine, a systems and lifestyle–based medical approach to address chronic disease. I had waited over three years to get to the point in my medical training when I could begin my formal education within the worlds of integrative and functional medicine. While I had been fortunate to meet functional pediatrician Dr. Karl Holtzer during my time in Pittsburgh back in May, I was now ready to see how my informal education compared to the comprehensive introductory course from the Institute for Functional Medicine (IFM).

When I first looked at the cost of the five-day training with the IFM earlier that year, I had felt defeated before the race had even begun. The price tag for the course was beyond my capacity as a medical student with no income. While my parents provided me with some extra money for living expenses so that I could use my roughly $50,000 in yearly loan money to cover tuition and avoid the next tier of higher-interest loans, I had little money to spare. After I scanned the IFM's website, I managed to find a somewhat buried page that opened up the possibility of a scholarship.

Could I get a scholarship to attend the training?

In response to my simple email inquiry—a hopeful wish from a student who needed help to begin his functional medicine education—I was offered a multi-thousand-dollar scholarship to attend the five-day training. While the scholarship would cover the program's tuition, I still needed a place to stay while I attended the training. I didn't even bother to look at hotels, which would likely be even less affordable than the five-day course. I called up a dear friend named Adrien Long instead. During my summer with Kelsey in 2015, I had spent several days with Adrien and his wife at my grandparents' lake house in North Carolina. We had bonded over our shared medical backgrounds, and I gravitated toward his youthful energy and intentional listening. Adrien wouldn't say no, and that was fine with me.

A few days before the training, I arrived at Adrien's in a state of unrelenting excitement. I jokingly told him that I was single again, and perhaps I would meet someone at the conference. During drives around his home near Towson and into downtown Baltimore, we bonded more and more through our shared vulnerability. Quite the fitness-oriented man himself, Adrien and I even attended a couple of group classes with his buddy Russ at their local gym. Adrien and I were not the kind for dull moments.

The first morning of the conference, I realized I was likely the youngest person in the room, and certainly looked it by perhaps ten years. As I walked around the tables of the conference hall, the truth was unavoidable: I was simply destined to be "that guy." Picking out a seat next to five other strangers, I couldn't help but wonder: *Where were the others like me?*

Where were the medical students and residents? Where were the young physicians interested in lifestyle medicine and root cause resolution approaches for addressing chronic disease? I understood the training's price barrier, but this was nuts! For an in-person training held only twice a year, how could I be the only attendee at my stage of education? While I had tremendous sympathy for the older physicians in attendance who wanted to resurrect their careers and find meaning once again after decades of fighting symptoms with medications, I just wasn't them. I didn't have decades of unfulfilling practice to unlearn.

As the week progressed, I was inundated with enough content to fill an entire semester. While I was certainly overwhelmed with information, I also recognized, despite my youth, that I possessed a wealth of knowledge and compassion to really help people—to truly assist them in finding their way. With each passing day, I felt less like a student and more like a physician who could guide his patients back to health. While I still had many months of school left before graduation, I no longer questioned if I could practice integrative medicine; I only questioned when.

While the program scholarship, the housing with Adrien, and the flexibility of my fourth-year curriculum were already miniature conspiring miracles that helped to manifest my medical dreams, my support from the universe was just getting started.

A few months before the IFM program in Baltimore, as part of my larger search for formal functional medicine education, I had discovered the newly developed ADAPT Clinician Training program created by my mentor, my ground zero: acupuncturist and researcher Chris Kresser. From his early podcasting days with The Healthy Skeptic in 2013, Chris had grown tremendously. Between work with patients in his California clinic and the expansion of his inquisitive podcast, Chris had started to train clinicians in functional and ancestral medicine using systems biology and an understanding of our evolutionary history. As part of a yearlong intensive training, Chris provided participants with not only the critical clinical skills necessary to practice functional medicine, but the practical business acumen to get it off the ground. With a price tag that included more digits than I had ever seen in my checking account, the financial investment was staggering. I approached my parents and shared with them the importance of this training to me, but the numbers were just so extraordinary. Undeterred by the obvious financial barrier, I composed a letter to Chris and his team so that they could understand my situation and truly see my heart.

Typing away on my laptop, I shared with Chris where I had come from and where I hoped to go. I let him know exactly how I had found him in the first place. I told him about my breaking and how I felt lucky to be alive at all. I really didn't need to tell him that I had no money—I was a medical student, and most medical students not only don't have money, they have what I like to call "negative money" in the form of debt and lost opportunity.

I asked if his team could provide the financial assistance that would be the only way I could afford his training.

After sending my email out into the ether, I stopped to say a prayer.

God, please tell him how much I need this. Please tell him how much I care.

Some days later, I received a response from Chris's team. They said they would consider an application for a scholarship. Within days of completing my application, I received another message from Chris's team.

I had a scholarship to take part in his training!

Many of you have likely heard the story about the man who started with a red paper clip and traded the paper clip for various new objects until he finally got to a house. With humility, curiosity, and a simple desire to never take no for an answer, I had found my way through multiple acts of immeasurable generosity, compassion, and unexplainable manifestation to the ability to pursue my dreams. Despite these obvious acts of divine manifestation and my conscious acknowledgment that I was receiving support from a realm I could not prove existed, however, I was human and could still accuse God, like the best of us, of having forgotten me.

≈ 41 ≈

Was God Still Listening?

San Francisco
November 2016

After my week of integrative medicine education in Baltimore, I returned to Charlottesville for my acting internship in outpatient family medicine, where I spent time with numerous family physicians within the UVA system. Grounded at home for more than a month, my mind turned back once again to exploring a romantic relationship.

Up to this point, I honestly had not had any bad experiences with online dating apps. Via Tinder, I had met Kelsey and had been able to grow without anger or resentment though my first relationship in years. Tinder also provided the opportunity to meet an authentic woman named Allie. Despite Allie's and my clear connection, the distance and directions for our lives pointed toward friendship, so we invested our energies and shared passions in a supportive platonic domain. While to that point I seemed to be winning at some aspects of the online dating game, September and the months beyond showed me why people avoid dating apps like the plague.

Over the course of several weeks, I connected with and made plans to meet three women. All three would either stand me up before our first meeting, reschedule for another meeting only to cancel again, or eventually disappear into the ether without a trace. Without knowing it, I had stumbled into the relational graveyard of ghosting, whereby individuals in emerging relationships vanish from existence without any communication or discussion as to why. For no rational reason, I had become a Casper magnet.

While two of the disappearances were at least marginally—and I mean marginally—explainable, the hardest one occurred in early November with a woman named Katie. Katie was a young occupational therapy student who lived about thirty minutes from Charlottesville in a town called Fishersville. After our connection online, we met in Charlottesville for a meal and eventually went on a hike. As I prepared to leave for a nearly four-week vacation that would take me across several parts of California for numerous residency interviews and a conference with the Mind & Life Institute that would celebrate the alchemy of neuroscience and mindfulness, I felt optimistic about our growing relationship and the evening phone conversations that were sure to come. With a final text to Katie before I departed from the Baltimore airport, little did I know that I would never hear from her again.

After I arrived in San Francisco, I made my way via trams and on foot to a small hostel that had gotten great reviews. At under $40 a night, my week in San Francisco would cost less than a single night in many of the area hotels. With a Trader Joe's nearby and a communal kitchen in the hostel, I was in heaven with all I needed to begin my exploration. I had essentially no plans while in San Francisco. I walked the city to explore its parks and trails and whatever else revealed itself to me. Averaging nearly twenty miles per day, I was one with my Osprey backpack and its water bottles tucked alongside.

One day, I decided to get adventurous and rented a bike to pick up some bigger miles as part of an adventure across the Golden Gate Bridge. I was an expert at solo adventures, and while this one provided a much needed break from medical school, I couldn't help but wonder, why was I always alone?

Why had another person disappeared from my life again?

Over the last two years, I had visited Roanoke, Staunton, Pittsburgh, Haiti, Baltimore, and now San Francisco. With the exception of the trip to Haiti, I had traveled solo and spent most of my time outside of any clinical and educational activities alone. As if my raging thoughts of loneliness and my questions for God needed any more steam, November 8, 2016, and its news broke on our lost world.

As day slipped into night, the media onslaught was clear: Donald Trump was on his way to being elected president of the United States of America. As this reality set in, San Francisco entered a state of turmoil. Needing to escape from the TV and its media bonanza, I sought out one of the tallest points in the city to completely embrace the unfolding. As I stared out into the fiery night and its sea of disbelief, my mind wanted to sink back into a dark oblivion. I asked God the ultimate question:

What do you want from me right now?

With all my miles walked through hurt and the complete disintegration of my being, I found it rather easy to imagine what our planet, with its hectares of humanity, could be feeling in this moment as we collectively struggled to discard the destructive illusion of separateness—from divinity, from self, from one another. Now accustomed to these emotional downpours, I was ready to take the metaphysical ensemble to the next level. I wanted to transmute my oppressive disillusionment and ask God to give me some answers.

Why the hell am I alone, God?

You gave me my life back to put me back into a growing hell? Was that the plan? I have the most beautifully preposterous vision to change the course of human healing, and I have no life partner, a mountain of debt, a generation of doctors who would rather I not exist, and not the faintest of road maps to construct a clinic for personalized love. How exactly do I relieve suffering when I have no fellow clinicians, no romantic partner in which to share in this miraculous splendor, and the world continues to polarize into unknowable chaos? Answer me please!

I had never been this demanding, this raw with God, but wasn't that precisely what this moment required? With at least an hour's walk between me and my hostel room, I pondered amid this abrupt release whether it was even worth it to go back or if I could find greater peace by simply sleeping under the stars. Before I could even look at this question through the lens of a rational mind, November softly whispered in my ear, "Get your ass home."

The next day I took the ferry to Angel Island to escape the emotional inferno that was the city. I walked around the island and learned about its history as an immigration station. After a climb to the top of the island to bear witness to the magical bay and the city across, I was filled with an unexpected sense of hope, a sense that I just needed to keep standing, to keep walking, to hold on to my enduring vision and faith. I may have felt lonely, but I was not alone. I may have been scared I would never actualize my functional medicine dreams, but I was not afraid. I may have felt I would never find my life partner, but I knew, in that moment, that she existed and was waiting for me the way I was waiting for her. I knew in that moment, that every single person who was meant to play a critical role in the creation of my heart's deepest vision was either already unknowingly in my life or soon to enter it as a family of hearts with unimaginable opportunity. God was asking for my continued manifestation and faith. And I was still willing to answer.

Part IV

Love and Letting Go

≈ 42 ≈

Finding Her

Outpatient Psychiatry
December 2016

After Thanksgiving break, I started a two-week rotation in outpatient psychiatry. Fascinated by the field of psychiatry minus its warped sense of medicating the human experience, I struggled quite mightily to find my path forward in medicine. While a career in family medicine had been stuck in my head since my return to school, I often felt more at home in the psychological realms and the complexity of the human psyche. Afraid that a psychiatry residency would destroy my sense of well-being faster than I could say "benzodiazepine," I stuck with family medicine and what seemed like the middle way.

On my first day of the rotation, I arrived at the outpatient clinic unsure exactly what to expect. I knew I would likely work with the resident psychiatrists, but I had no idea what my role or the expectations of students would be. Greeting some of the residents, I realized that I had met many of them as second-years back during my third-year hospital psychiatry rotation. While I spotted some new faces mixed in with the familiar, I felt at home with this group and was eager to help the patients we would see together.

About halfway into my first morning, after working with one of the main resident physicians, I decided to expand my experience by moving on to another resident doctor. As I walked out of his office and into another hallway, I found that there was only one other door open. Unsure which resident was working behind the cracked entryway, I took the opportunity simply because I wanted to avoid the disruption of knocking on a closed office door.

As I pushed upon the door, I was greeted by a face I already knew—one that had changed very little since our first encounter nearly a year earlier. The resident was none other than Selene! After I asked quite sheepishly if she would mind me tagging along for her next clinical encounter, she invited me to sit before the next patient arrived.

She was just as quiet, mysterious, and unmistakably beautiful as on our first day in the hospital, and my mind couldn't help but unravel again into tumultuous curiosity. As I looked around her office, I got a sense of her artistic and creative nature. Seeing the intermingled symbolism of the chakra system amid elements of Buddhist and Hindu spirituality, I started to imagine what she loved outside of her work.

My daydream just beginning, I was brought back to reality by the creak of the door and the entrance of her patient. As I sat tucked away in my chair, trying to be more invisible than even a fly on the wall, I watched as Selene listened and paused to reflect on the patient's concerns. With the understanding that medication had massive limitations, Selene's carefully chosen words and focus on building a psychotherapeutic relationship brought relief to a human engulfed in emotional chaos. While I had little evidence to prove my developing theory, I had a strong sense that the other residents did not speak, let alone think, like Selene. Because she was stuck in a system that glorified medicating the human experience, I could already sense that Selene recognized the importance of exploring therapies outside of medication and that she was more like me than perhaps any other resident I had ever met.

As the session wrapped up, Selene walked the patient out and we prepared for the next encounter. No matter the opportunities that awaited me with the other nine residents, I just wanted to sit with Selene and continue to take all of her in.

After I got back to my apartment later that evening, I could not get Selene out of my head.

Who was she? Where had she come from? Does she meditate as her room and artwork suggested? I wonder if she's married? Married? Are you out of your goddamn mind?

And so it went.

For the next week, I returned each day to spend more time with the psychiatry residents. Despite the opportunity to learn from all of the young doctors, I spent more and more time with Selene. By the end of the week, I could no longer deny my fascination.

While I was not yet friends with any of the residents, I had grown closer with a vivacious and always joyful resident named Jackie. Jackie was also a more holistically minded clinician—a genuine human being who deeply cared about her work. She spent lots of extra time answering my many questions and helped me engage with some of her patients. While most of my queries were focused on our specific patient encounters or connected to something I had learned in school, eventually I asked something I never thought would come out of my mouth.

"Are you friends with Selene?" I wondered aloud.

Immediately reading between the lines, Jackie replied in step, "Yes, pretty good. Why do you ask?"

"Well, she seems very spiritual and into meditation, but really quiet and kind of mysterious."

Before Jackie could ask further about my specific interests, I got straight to the point.

"Is she married or does she have a boyfriend?"

"I'm not sure," she replied, "but I can try to find out for you if you would like?"

"That would be amazing!"

"Of course. I'll see what I can do."

The walk home that evening was essentially a run.

I bet she's single, and I can try to talk to her. Maybe we can be friends and meditate together. Who knows what could happen after that?

And off I went again.

The next day I made a beeline for Jackie. I needed my answer and I needed it now.

"Well, she doesn't sound like she's seeing anyone, so you should try to talk to her. You never know . . ."

As the specifics of this answer settled in, I felt an immediate anxiety about the ridiculousness of this situation.

I mean she's a doctor, and I am a student. This kind of plotline doesn't even happen in Grey's Anatomy *let alone real life.*

The inner torment was unlike anything I had ever felt before. If I had been filled with these kinds of thoughts upon my return to school, I would have never even considered them. If they had entered my head even one year earlier, I would have laughed off my bravado. If they had arrived just six months earlier, I would have only played out the next encounter in the sea of my mind. But here I was now, considering talking to her and seeking out a friendship and whatever else could flow from a simple act of faith.

I never had a steady girlfriend in high school. After my freshman year of college, I barely spoke to a woman with an interest at dating or a romantic relationship. Over the past two years I had made some progress in dating, but all of these women had at least expressed some interest in me. This would be different. This would be doing something I never imagined I could do. It was madness.

As the two-week rotation came to a close, I needed to make a plan to tell Selene just how I felt. After my last day in the outpatient clinic, Selene was scheduled to be on the hospital consult service, a duty the ten residents shared in order to cover the weekend days. She would be at the hospital alone—no other residents or distractions, just her.

I decided to write her a card and bring her some tea. At the outpatient clinic, she always seemed to have some kind of tea, and I figured she would appreciate the gesture and small gift. While at my local farmers market early Saturday morning, I explored the options for cards and tea. Next to my friend's kombucha booth, I found an herb and tea stand with the hilarious name of "Profani-teas." The owners gave each tea hand-crafted from herbs grown in their own gardens a quirky name with a profane kicker. From "Calm the Fuck Down" to "Get the Fuck Over It," the names and the teas themselves were just perfect. Falling myself for the alluring smell and depth of "Get the Fuck Over It," I bought it and a card with which to share my heart with Selene.

Selene's shift ended around 5 p.m. So I planned to meet her with my card and tea sometime after 4. Walking into the hospital on a Saturday afternoon, I recognized that I could have been as far away from this place as I wanted, but here I was again, with the hospital exactly where I wanted to be.

During my climb up to the psychiatry unit on the fifth floor, I realized I had a problem—or should I say a few problems.

First, I didn't actually have Selene's phone number. I had no way to communicate directly with her to find out where she was. Second, I was now just remembering from my third-year psychiatry days that the hospital unit where the psychiatry residents generally stayed required a student ID and an additional tool for entry—a key. I no longer had such a key. The weight of humiliation was starting to set in.

What a stupid idea. Give up now and go back home with some of your pride intact.

With such thoughts beginning to unravel me, I got out of my head and reached out to God.

What in the world am I supposed to do?

In this new state of surrender, with a tear or two trying to spill down my cheek and onto the third-floor stairwell, I collected myself.

What do you have to lose? Just walk up to the fifth floor, step around the corner near the psychiatry unit entrance, and just see. You could even wait for five or ten minutes and see if she comes out. You have nothing to lose. Just walk up to the fifth floor.

I scaled the final two flights and went around the final corner to the psychiatric unit entrance. Several yards away stood a slender figure in green scrubs. The woman was looking down at a sheet of paper and had just clipped her pager back to her pants. As I stepped closer, she raised her head and our eyes met.

It was Selene.

Somehow, someway, she was here.

"What are you doing here on the weekend?" she asked.

After pausing for a second, I replied, "I came to find you."

In that moment, Selene's face turned from confusion to disbelief. She did not know what to say.

"I have one final consult in the ER. It's been a really long day, but if you want to wait, I can talk to you afterward in the consultation room. Here's my number. Just send me a text, and I will message you when I'm done and can let you in."

Not sure what to think yet, I entered her number into my phone and confirmed that she had received my message. She then walked into the elevator and was whisked down to the ER.

Will she actually message me? Where do I wait? Will it take an hour? She actually gave me her number. What is going on?

I eventually walked back down the flight of stairs and to the medical school. From there I went to the nursing school to meditate and even do some yoga. As the minutes ticked by, I bounded back and forth between impatient excitement and anxiety that this was not real.

An hour later, I got a text from Selene. She was back in the consulting room. I could meet her there, and she would let me in. Basically sprinting from the nursing school back to the main hospital, I found my way to the consulting room and inside to be with her.

She was visibly fatigued, sweating, and tired beyond measure. I could tell she had had a rough day and just wanted to finish her last note so she could go home. After she put the last keystrokes together on her final consult, she logged off the computer and turned to look at me. Unsure where exactly to start, I just jumped into an expression of my gratitude.

"I just wanted to thank you for all the time you gave me during my rotation. I know having med students is probably annoying, and it meant a lot to me to be able to spend some time with you."

As I finished my trembling words, she took the card from my hand and opened it. Reading through the lines, she started to cry.

"This is so thoughtful, Rob. You really didn't need to do this."

Staring back at her grateful, teary eyes, I realized I had somehow managed to manifest another unexpected problem. Still within my hands and obvious to see was a little box, the tea I had purchased at the market. Now you would think that the gift of tea would never be an issue, but this wasn't just any kind of tea. It was Profani-tea.

As the moment unfolded, Selene looked at me and said that the card alone was too much. She didn't expect any gifts and she was simply grateful that I had come to the hospital to see her. With the opportunity now to navigate away from the final gift if I wanted, I pondered one last time: should I still give her the tea? I held out the tea box and then held my breath for what could have been the end before the beginning. As she read the label of "Get the Fuck Over It," she stayed quiet for what seemed like the world's longest pause.

Finally, as she looked up and stared into my eyes, she said, "Thank you—this is exactly what I need to do."

After wiping away a tear, she opened the box to smell what was inside. Now smiling, she thanked me, and we both rested in the pleasure of our authentic human interaction. In a tiny room hidden inside of a massive hospital, one doctor and one medical student, through collective acts of courage and emotional expression, sought to shift the world back into its seat of love, two giant leaps of faith at a time.

After a few minutes of final reflection, Selene collected her things, and we made our way out of the hospital. As we reached the front lobby, I turned toward her to give her a hug. She accepted my embrace. As I stepped away, I looked one more time into her eyes.

"Thank you," she said.

And we walked our separate ways into the distant night.

43

Rumi's Love

Durham, North Carolina, and Charlottesville
December 2016

By this point in my fourth year of school, I had completed several interviews at family medicine residency programs across the country. In an effort to find the best place for my future training, I was beyond calm and saw the interviews more as tours than professional auditions. With my résumé and grades, I could go almost anywhere I wanted—anywhere perhaps, except one place.

The family medicine program at Duke was routinely ranked in the top ten in the country and boasted some of the most accomplished and diverse doctors in the world. As it was one of the only medical centers on the East Coast with an integrative medicine focus, I was eager to see if Duke could be a home for me.

While I had never visited Duke's campus, Durham and the medical center were not entirely new ground. Just over twenty-six years earlier, my mother gave birth to my twin brother and me, many weeks premature, in Duke's prestigious hospital. After calling the NICU home for several weeks, we were discharged with no roadblocks in our way. While my family moved to Virginia soon after our birth, I could not deny that Durham was a place that remained in my heart as part of our origin story.

I made the multihour drive to Durham late one Wednesday evening, feeling for the very first time a sense of nervousness, a sense of uncertainty. With my California vacation still fresh in my mind, intermingled neuronally with the mystery of Selene close by, I started to wonder what I really wanted for my future. I was convinced just weeks ago that a California adventure could be the next stage of my life. Then came Selene. And now Duke. I had worked toward this moment for over eight years. All of my academic efforts in college and medical school—even high school for that matter—were culminating now in this final choice for my professional pursuits.

Just as I arrived at my hotel in Durham, I got a message from my friend and former roommate Thomas Ball. Thomas asked if I wanted to attend a celebration of the mystic poet Rumi later that weekend. He was planning to go with his girlfriend and thought I would enjoy the event, too. Immediately thinking of Selene, I imagined a celebration of romanticism and mystery with her by my side. There was just one problem: I hadn't heard from her in four days. I had sent her daily messages of hope and some of my personal poems, but I had not yet received any communication since our last meeting at the hospital.

After I found my room, I put away a couple things and double-checked the schedule for my interview the next day. With the logistics confirmed, my mind turned back once again to Selene.

How was her week going? Was she okay?

I thought about sending her another message as I lay in bed, but what was the point? I had already sent four or five without a reply.

As if responding to my mental inquiries, at that moment my phone alerted me to a text message—it was from her! In the text she said how much she appreciated my messages and poems throughout the week. She had been busy, a little overwhelmed, and not quite sure exactly how to respond to me. She also said that while she was not in a romantic relationship, she thought all she could do at this point was pursue a friendship with me.

While the last part of her message could have been massively deflating, I was just overjoyed to hear from her. At first I was not sure whether I should reply immediately or give things some time. But I realized that hours were slipping away and my interview day would be busy. I needed to ask her to the Celebration of Rumi right now.

The next morning, I woke up to a new message from Selene.

"Yes, that sounds wonderful. I would like to join you."

While I was never really a coffee person—relying instead on green and herbal tea—her message alone was like a double espresso followed by a liter of Mountain Dew. I was exhilarated and couldn't quite understand my luck.

By the end of my day of interviews, I was amazed at the level of excellence and drive of both the residents and the faculty. Duke was indeed a stunning place, but would it become a stunning place for me?

Friday crawled by, but Saturday, December 17, 2016, finally arrived with the promise of seeing Selene again. We had exchanged a few messages over the last two days to ensure that she knew the location of the event and how to get there. With only a short drive across town, I arrived some minutes early and shortly before Thomas and his girlfriend, Zona.

After I stepped inside, I texted Selene to let her know I was there. I saved a seat next to me, but the minutes ticked by with still no Selene. At 4 o'clock with the celebration soon to begin, Selene hadn't arrived.

As people waited for the organizers' first introduction, Selene texted me to say that she had just arrived but the entrance was locked. Did I know where to get in? Confused, as the main doors had been wide open just minutes prior, I did not know how to respond. A minute or so later, she still couldn't get in and was thinking about going home. I had to find her and get her into the building. Standing now, I peered from a window and spotted Selene. Dressed in white, she was walking around the outside of the building trying to find a way inside. I went to the front of the building to find a way to get her in. Just as another woman stepped inside, I saw several people on their way to the door with Selene not far behind. I called out and told her I had seats for the two of us. She had made it. We had made it. It was time for the show to begin.

The next two hours were nearly indescribable. With music, dancing, singing, poetry, storytelling, and prayer, the event engaged in a communal act of love. Although our gathering may have centered on the celebration of a Sufi mystic, the celebration commemorated the life and love of all humans alike.

During a portion of the celebration that showcased the beauty of the Whirling Dervishes, we all joined in, dancing joyfully. Watching Selene move about the room, dressed in white, was like watching an angel float amid mere humans. It was as if she were incapable of leaving footprints.

After the celebration we decided to take a walk to a nearby Thai restaurant. While we had spent a short time together in the hospital just a few days before, this was the first time we had faced each other, eye to eye, without any medical responsibilities to cloud the air.

"I remember when you spoke out in grand rounds. I thought you were a little crazy, but it's starting to make a little more sense now," she shared with a chuckle.

"I guess I can be a little opinionated and opposed to the hierarchy," I chimed back with a smile. "It's funny, psychiatry was my last third-year clerkship and the only one where I got an A. I did pretty average on the shelf exam, but got a couple honors evaluations so I think Dr. Henderson must have felt sorry for me or something and just decided to give me an A."

"Well, I didn't really understand you. You would always be gone when we were trying to start rounds, but you seemed to actually care about the patients so I couldn't really get upset. You were kind of a gunner, but you also didn't seem to care what the attendings thought of you, so basically you didn't make any sense. I actually wrote one of those honors evaluations for you."

"What?" I spurted, almost spitting out my curry.

"Yeah. I think I only did like two or three of those evaluations all year. It's way too much work for that nonsense."

When the meal was finally over, we walked outside again to enjoy more of the evening.

With the college students gone for winter break, Charlottesville was bathed in calm for the first time in over five months. Walking the peaceful streets around campus, we took in some of the cool starlit evening and some of the wonder of which Rumi spoke so fondly. While I could have spent the entire night with her underneath the stars, we eventually needed to say goodbye. I walked Selene back to her car and prepared to send her off into the night once more. Standing outside of her car, I stumbled significantly to find my final words.

"Selene, I don't know if I can do this. I am already falling in love with you, and there is so much uncertainty in my life right now."

With little hesitation, Selene responded, "It's okay. I feel the same way. Just try not to think so much," she whispered back with a smile.

I felt a sense of peace with her reassuring reply and walked back to my car parked a few yards away.

Into the night we drove, with only God knowing what would happen next.

⁓ 44 ⁓

Where Do We Go from Here?

Greensboro, North Carolina, and Charlottesville
December 2016

The next morning I messaged Selene to let her know how much I had enjoyed our time together and that I had yet another residency interview in Greensboro, North Carolina, the following day. With two more interviews scheduled before Christmas, I still had miles of pavement to traverse on the residency interview journey. In response to my text, Selene asked if I wanted to come over to her apartment that afternoon after church and before my drive to Greensboro. When I looked up her address, I realized she lived just a mile from my church.

Where, God, would things go from here?

With only a few minutes from the church parking lot to her front door, I had little time to overthink the next steps in our unfolding connection. After I arrived at a complex surprisingly filled with nature, I found her apartment nestled near some trees and knocked on her door. I heard a dog barking inside. As I tried to decipher the elements of the bark and predict what kind of dog it could be, Selene answered the door with a pair of dog eyes peering from behind her leg. She let me in, warning at the same time that Xena, a Shar-Pei and English bulldog mix, would likely bark quite a bit. Now inside, I embraced Xena's version of a hug.

Selene motioned me to a couch, I sat down next to her to take off where we had ended the night before. As I listened to the stories from the many books she was constantly reading, I stepped further and further into the spiritually synchronistic world that was Selene's mind. Because she was an artist at heart, I saw myself wrapped inside of her soul, just trying in her own way to find the love and wonder hidden in the world. In between her stories and our time lost in books, I met the rest of her menagerie that included a long-haired Chihuahua named Cujo, a pitch-black cat named Misa, a Sphynx cat named Rem, and a cuddly chinchilla named Pikachu. For a two-bedroom apartment, she had quite the zoo.

After what seemed like only minutes, the hands of her clock told me it was time to say goodbye. I had a number of hours to drive before reaching yet another random hotel, so I packed up my backpack and tossed it over my shoulder. With the front door still open, I swiveled away to head back to my car. There was just one thing—

I wasn't ready to leave.

I stood rooted within the small garden outside of her apartment, consumed by one thought and one thought only.

If you don't go back in there right now and kiss her, you will never make it to Greensboro and you may never make it through this life at all.

As I continued to stall and ponder the immensity of what such a gesture would mean, I was paralyzed by the fear of not being well received and ruining everything we had worked thus far to create, the fear of missing out on what I had waited so long to finally unearth.

In spite of all that, I stepped back through the doorway and moved forward to embrace Selene. As I brought my lips a mere inch from her face, I realized without words that she was thinking the exact same thing, too. Forgetting the reveries I had been fighting since that day we had first met, I completely surrendered to what currently was. Lost for a time in the eruption of our embrace, I eventually paused for a moment to finally remember the details of my current situation. I still had to leave to get to Greensboro for my interview.

Fucking Greensboro.

Just as quickly as the passion had erupted, I was forced to say goodbye. Despite the need to leave something so raw, so poetically beautiful, I knew what had just been born in this simple apartment in Charlottesville, and surely, I could wait a couple days to get back to the presence of the person for whom I had been waiting my entire life.

45

Four Years

Geriatrics
February 2017

As Selene's and my relationship sped forward, I could hardly believe the latest turns my life had taken. It had now been four years since the lowest point in my life. I had persevered through every relational and educational hardship and was now mere months away from graduation. While I had been knocked down into holes where everything seemed impossible, the impossible was now all I chose to believe.

As part of the bizarre transition from medical school to residency, fourth-year students across the country participate in a spectacle known as "The Match." After weeks and weeks of interviews where residency programs of all kinds assessed the caliber of their potential candidates and residents explored which programs and lifestyles would best fit their needs for the next three to seven years, the entire dance culminated in the programs and students collectively entering their individual preference into a massive algorithmic matching system.

Just weeks before the algorithm's selections are revealed, students submit an ordinal list of their top residency programs with their first choice as number 1. While the selection process is often remarkably nerve-racking for students—with radical experiments in game theory well on display—I never expected my own selections to carry such intensity, such a weight of the unknown.

After almost fifteen residency interviews, I had discovered two important things. First, I recognized that Duke was arguably the best program and met many of my interests. The program was also relatively close to Selene and my Charlottesville family and provided access to a formal integrative medicine practice. Second, I understood that I was a top candidate at essentially every program other than Duke. As I played through hundreds of different scenarios, I ultimately realized that if I picked any program other than Duke first, I was essentially guaranteed to match. In addition, even if I picked Duke first, but did not match with them, I would ultimately be paired with whatever program I picked second.

So where did I want to go? Did I want to give Duke a shot?

Back in November I had been ready for a California adventure. By December I had my eyes turned toward Duke. By February, I didn't know which way was up. While it had only been three months since our first encounter as a couple, I loved every minute of my growing relationship with Selene. The idea of living in California, which seemed so real just a few months earlier, now struck me as completely untenable. To move away from Selene was something my heart would not allow.

With the West Coast off the table, I looked at other programs closer to home. While I had a number of choices from my interview season, I narrowed the options down to two. Connected with the newly formed Cleveland Clinic Center for Functional Medicine, the Cleveland Clinic's family medicine residency program seemed quite progressive and a wonderful fit for my professional endeavors. With its cold winters and a seven-hour drive from Charlottesville, however, I was not entirely sure my heart could handle either the weather or the distance.

My second option was a rural, academically affiliated program in Winchester, Virginia. Located about two hours from Charlottesville, the program was relatively small with only five individuals per class and offered the ability for more engagement with supervising physicians as compared to overloaded teaching hospitals. The program also boasted a few key individuals with passions for integrative medicine and psychology. While choosing a nonacademic program might seem odd, I honestly wanted a different experience from the academic rigors I had known at UVA. Academia had served its purpose for my medical schooling, but residency would be an entirely different situation. I was not interested in what I had witnessed at UVA or other programs housed within similarly confining walls.

In addition to the opportunity for more intimate teaching environments, the program in Winchester was within driving distance of Selene and my Charlottesville church community. At the suggestion of some dear medical school classmates back in 2014, I had started to attend Cornerstone Community Church. Inside a building complex that looked more like a storefront than a church, I had discovered a collection of souls and faith that I had never known existed. In a worship group led by Tucker MacDonald, I found warmth and love with progressive music and the practical words of Pastor Tony Schiavone.

While I could have certainly ended up at any church in Charlottesville and felt some sense of connection to grow my faith, Cornerstone was where my heart deeply longed to be.

Throughout the years of medical school, Cornerstone had become a foundation in my life. In the summer of 2016 I had even chosen to be baptized—a conscious spiritual commitment that represented so much more than my christening as a young child. Having lived most of my life without much spiritual direction, the baptism felt like the perfect way to proclaim my faith and connection with my community. As part of that growing commitment, I had served in the youth ministry with elementary school kids. Expanding from my time in 2013 when I taught at an after-school program and oversaw kids at a YMCA summer camp, I found great peace with the creative play of children. While my evolving mindfulness practice, the changes to my dietary and exercise habits, and even my conscious social explorations were critical lifestyle decisions that had helped me restore and improve my health, the creative play, faith, and presence of these children were possibly the most instrumental elements in the flourishing of my spirit.

If life involved decisions made inside a vacuum, things would be rather simple. Professional endeavors would be informed by the best professional choice, travel by the most affordable and available options, partners perhaps by the most suitable people who live close by—but that's not how life works. When you start a residency, you are not just choosing a place to work, but also a place to live, to laugh, to cry, to grow a family, to grow faith. While I didn't have children or anything objectively that tied me to any one location, my heart was beginning to feel pangs at the potential for heartbreak.

Could I really move away from Charlottesville, away from Selene, away from my church community? Could I really move away from the life I had reconstructed after years of loss after loss after loss?

While the UVA family medicine residency program did not fit my professional and lifestyle interests, I didn't want to leave my joyful life in Charlottesville behind.

As I struggled to discern attachment from realistic relational connections, I cried and cried, at a loss as to what I should do. Eventually I sat down with Selene to make sense of it all. As she herself had gone through the matching process as a surgical resident a few years before, she was intimately aware of the mind games involved and the aching in my heart.

While we explored my options, I shared with her my desire to continue growing our relationship and how I wanted in every way to foster our emerging love. No longer considering the West Coast programs, I was able to whittle down the ultimate options that had been on my mind. Given my interests and concerns with Duke, I asked her if our relationship would make it if I matched in Durham. My heart felt like it already knew her answer, but my practical mind just didn't know if the distance would drive us apart. With little hesitation, she told me that we could make anything work and to not keep it off my list because of how far it was from Charlottesville. With her simple act of loving commitment, my hours of deliberation finally came to an end. I was going to give Duke a shot—so what would be number 2?

I honestly can't tell you what went through my mind as I clicked the mouse to make my second and remaining selections, but I ultimately knew that the outcome didn't matter. I would show up to the moment and love what was in front of me.

～ 46 ～

The Match

Sports Medicine
March 2017

The Match was here, and the celebrations were on. While I technically had six weeks of school left to complete, The Match was the first ritualistic transition from medical student to resident doctor. Selene had left for a two-week trip in Egypt, but my father drove up to share in the schoolwide spectacle. Just four years earlier, he had made the exact same drive to meet me in the hospital as a patient who had no idea if he would ever make it back to school at all.

In the large auditorium where The Match would happen, I sat with my dear friend Thomas Ball to await our next steps. While Thomas and I had started school together with the original class of 2016, we had both taken a year off before returning to finish in 2017. As each student was called up one by one to be given a sealed letter that held their fate, friends and family cheered us on as we all waited for the big reveal.

After over 160 envelopes were handed out, we were given the final go-ahead from our medical school deans to open the letters. Massive eruptions cascaded around the room as individuals discovered their residency future. I paused, eyes closed to take a few deep breaths.

Then, I removed the letter and unfolded it.

As I read down to the ultimate decision, I took in what God had planned for me: Valley Health Shenandoah Family Practice Residency; Winchester, Virginia.

Duke, it turned out, did not have eyes on me.

I felt a funny sense of relief and understanding with God. My work in Charlottesville, despite the upcoming move to Winchester, was not about to end.

I walked out to find my dad and show him the letter that held my future.

"Well, I guess that just proves we are a UNC family."

Indeed we are, Dad. Indeed we are.

47

When the Mind and the Soul Make Love

Introduction to Psychoanalysis
March 2017

After The Match, my life accelerated. With aspects of my future now solidified, I embraced my free time to explore the next phase of my compassionate revolution. With the Mindfulness Practice Schedule email and my work with CALM, I had been given a template, a community of like-minded souls to grow our collective efforts, but now I wanted to create something entirely new, something entirely on my own.

But would anyone actually give a shit?

With Selene still in Egypt, I decided to meditate to strengthen our energetic connection and ease my aching heart. Dropping the desire to immediately find a name for my incubating creative endeavor, I set my focus on my breath and a visualization of her world. Helped by pictures from her astonishing adventure, I drew closer and closer to her spiritual being thousands of miles away.

As the connection deepened, I visualized her face and a radiant halo around her being. Without reason, without rational intention, I felt a sense of beauty and awe at the power of my mind to connect me with her enduring presence of love. As I sought to rest with this powerful image for a few moments, I was struck with the words "A Beautiful Mind."

Floodgates opened, my attention turned to the remembrance of the hauntingly intense movie by the same name. Drawn into the residue of beauty, awe, and relative disbelief that the movie engendered alongside the image of my partner with her radiant soul, I spoke aloud, "a beautiful mind, a beautiful mind." Immersed in a state of pure ecstasy at this simple, but overwhelming revelation, I felt the name of my mission dance straight off my tongue.

A Medicinal Mind

After an intellectual pivot to further define the word *medicinal*, I uncovered synonyms such as *curative*, *healing*, *therapeutic*, and *restorative*. As each word passed over me like a sweet summer cloud, I felt a sense of energetic calm, a confirmation that I had finally found the name. Through all of my own healing, my writing, my poetry, and even my conversations with patients, through the often painful solo travels to different parts of the world, what I had wanted more than anything else for every being on this planet was to unearth and preserve "a medicinal mind"—a therapeutic, contemplative, and loving mind.

As Viktor Frankl so eloquently reminded us through the telling of his own horrific walk through life in a WWII concentration camp, the mind and your perspective can always remain yours, even when everything else has been stripped off and thrown away. While we may never live in a society without hate and violence, we can always work to curate a mind that rests in the beds of faith and joy, even when the world is lost and cannot find its way.

~ 48 ~

The First Words

Introduction to Psychoanalysis
March 2017

With the incorporation of photographs from my brother and my dear friend Max Mishkin, A Medicinal Mind became a centralized website for the exploration of curious love, constructed by a "family" that understood its deep intentions. While I had been stealthily inserting some of my poems into the Mindfulness Practice Schedule weekly emails and had even received messages of appreciation from readers, I had yet to put my name to my emotional wanderings. A Medicinal Mind would finally become their home.

Back in October 2016, I had attended an integrative medicine forum in Washington DC known as the Functional Forum. As part of the gathering, I met a longtime mentor in the space of integrative medicine named James Maskell. James was an incredibly tall figure, and simply being in his presence was like standing beside a redwood tree. Despite his physical overshadowing of my 5'8" frame, I felt no hierarchical power, only James's deep appreciation for a medical student aligned with the mission of functional and integrative medicine.

As we talked and shared aspects of our unique life stories, I told James about my working list of educational resources constructed over my years of informal "education" into integrative and functional medicine. From books and podcasts to blogs and online videos, I had discovered an overwhelming number of resources to grow my integrative medicine education alongside my formal medical school training. With the end of medical school just months away, my list of resources languished on an overburdened laptop just waiting for a "baterrial" explosion.

James immediately saw the true treasure that lived beneath my keyboard and expressed his desire to share my collected resources as an educational e-book for his audience and to record a podcast together about the e-book's intention and my unique story. Stunned by his invitation and generosity, I could no longer deny my unfolding path as a guide, a messenger, a storyteller for the way we, as humans, can heal.

After I returned home from the event that would arguably become one of the most momentous days of my entire life, I ran into an unexpected hurdle.

What in the hell do I use to make an e-book?

After a few Google searches and some technological despair, I decided to try the Pages application on my Apple laptop. Within minutes, I had fallen into a dance of copy, paste, link insertion, and photo cropping. With a seemingly endless pool of photographs from James and Max, the e-book morphed from a text wasteland into something I would dare call art. *The Functional and Integrative Medicine Education Resource* became a communal creation with an author that could only cry at the improbability of it all.

While the power of the written word—whether through a poem, the e-book, or a narrative blog—could pour forth from me as ripples of my awakening soul, the educational form that had brought me out of the depths, that had filled my mind for days throughout medical school, was the auditory splendor of a podcast. With earbuds and a street or trail beneath my feet, I logged thousands of miles and accumulated arguably more pertinent and expansive wisdom through my hours of listening than I did through my formal medical training. Podcasts were a unifier, an elevater, a journey of expansive inquiry. With my interest in extensive locomotion, audio was the perfect media to expand my worlds of healing and contemplative practice.

Perhaps it's hard to get my fascination and obsession with podcasts. Perhaps if you haven't had your life awakened, your life's purpose realized through a simple audio file, my fascination will only ever appear to be a crazed obsession. Soaking up knowledge and insight from as many flowers and green spaces as possible, I held no allegiances or grudges, just curiosity into the beauty of the healing way. While these "butterfly years" of podcasts were a necessary piece of my medical education journey, no one can stay in the womb of education forever. As you internalize a growing amount of new information, you will inevitably start to more critically evaluate what it is you have actually soaked up from the world. As I progressed beyond awe and excitement at the acquisition of new knowledge, I became more discerning of the ideas that sought a new home in my curious mind space. From a place of respectful critique, I did not immediately accept a podcaster's comments as guaranteed fact and instead developed my own opinions, views, and insights that yearned to find a voice out in the crowded world.

While I could easily squeeze out this sponge of knowledge in the form of my very own medical podcast, the world certainly didn't need me to spit thrice-baked ideas into an echo chamber. The greatest gift I could squeeze from my sponge was not the knowledge I had gleaned, but the empowerment to look at the human experience in expansive new ways. In order to achieve this end, I wanted to create a podcast that shared knowledge *and* stories, deeply human stories. I wanted to find the divine within others, so I could reflect back the divine within me. I wanted to find the spiritual vegetables hidden within the medical meat loaf. It was time to get a microphone and some friends to start it all.

ॐ 49 ॐ

The Origins of Suffering

Somewhere in Charlottesville
March–May 2017

During Selene's spiritual journey in Egypt, I lived in her apartment and cared for our little zoo. As I tended to the needs of the animals amid my own creative incubation, I prayed each night that the animals would remain well and that Selene would return home safely. After an impossibly long two weeks, Selene stepped off the train still beaming with radiance from the African sun.

As I embraced her for what felt like the first time our beings had ever touched, I could finally step out of the uncertainty around her safe travels and the lives of our joyful zoo. Uncertainty is a funny thing. One of the biggest drivers of fear and a destroyer of love, uncertainty—with its lack of control and discomfort—has destroyed more lives, more divine lights than any pestilence in the history of the world. Take away a man's sustenance and he will remain on the search for food until his body can't breathe any longer, but take away a man's connection to his divine nature and he will accelerate his physical destruction for it appears to be the only way to actually return to the lost divine.

Beginning with my own near-death experience and awakening, I had moved through medical school as a curious observer of how health care treated "death." We were taught in many ways as if death were the ultimate failure, the ultimate act of suffering for the individual and their loved ones. Death and its attached suffering in the view of medical professionals were to be avoided at all costs.

No matter how admirable it seemed to save the life of an individual in a terrible car accident, however; I couldn't help but look at death as the transition back to God as anything but divine.

How could death be a failure? How could death actually be worse than living on a ventilator as your physical form erodes in an ICU during the middle of the night with your family far away?

Death couldn't be a failure.

Sometimes I have wondered if our maniacal efforts at preserving life at all costs are partly a reaction to all the lives lost through suicide, through black holes that sucked out the divine light, the divine energy in a being such that they could no longer see its radiance. Suicide has been called the ultimate act of "selfishness," yet it is only through the complete dissolution of the inner divine light, the truth of the divine self, that anyone would ever be capable of prematurely ending their human existence. Through this lens, we see that, indeed, not only is suicide not "selfish," it is arguably the ultimate act of *"self-LESS-ness"*—a loss of the divine self so severe that it leads to the destruction of the human form.

As I reflected more and more on the medical road ahead of me, I imagined the lives of the patients that would intersect with my own. All in states of relative suffering, many patients would surely be at the last bus stop before death, and others still would be too scared to get on the bus itself. I would find patients who were struggling to keep the divine light bright within their hearts, while others would be destructively overwhelmed by its radiance.

I knew without actually articulating it that the conversations that lay ahead for me about life, death, meaning, suffering, pain, and uncertainty could not be avoided, nor could they be judged as any more or less important than any of my "medical" tasks. I wouldn't have the chance to observe and learn from my mentors' conversations at death's door, yet I had to have them. I knew without knowing that 2020 was on the horizon and the pursuit of unconditional love before this torment could not be forsaken.

In the final weeks before graduation, I met a young black man, muscular and grizzled, playing the most beautiful piano music I had ever heard in the UVA Medical Center lobby. I watched as his creative vibrations evaporated the despair emanating from nearby hospital halls. Stepping up to the piano after the completion of his improvised sound, I shared simple words of gratitude.

"I've been here for almost five years and never heard music like that. Thank you for sharing your gifts."

"Oh, I was just kind of messing around, but thank you for listening!"

"My name's Rob."

"Devin. Nice to meet you."

After one further improvised melody, I asked Devin if he wanted to go get some food and share in more conversation. As he was without steady income, it simply made sense to go share in a meal together and to be a light in some way for Devin just as he had been an unexpected light to me.

Because of this conscious choice to spend time with Devin, I missed a sports medicine clinic that was part of my school elective obligations. Weeks later, amid my final medical school evaluations, I became aware that my sports medicine preceptor had contemplated failing me for this unprofessional act, which would have left me without the necessary credits to graduate. While I can't deny that my choice to spend time with Devin and other previous decisions like this went against the numerous expectations of me as a medical student, I couldn't help but feel that with every "controversial" decision I made, my ultimate acts of human expression were precisely what was required in each moment. Since I accepted and took responsibility for my chosen actions, I held no resentment for those who viewed them as selfish, unprofessional, or immature; in their minds they were "right" to the extent that "right" was even possible.

With each choice, each miniature act of human rebellion, I realized that the road ahead in residency would not be certain, would not be comfortable, and most certainly would not be within my control. No matter what I would face, however, I vowed to keep the divine light within me lit and return to my anchors of contemplation, prayer, and the acts of self-love that Selene and so many had allowed me to deeply and infinitely live.

50

Closing a Chapter

Medical School Graduation
May 2017

By the time May rolls around in your final year of medical school, most graduating students are transfixed by the massive transition ahead into residency. With tremendous responsibility and financial, albeit inadequate, compensation on the horizon, the "practicals" of finding a place to live, moving, and grounding oneself in a new professional unknown would have been the logical things to ponder. My mind, as you already know, did not regularly fixate on the "practicals."

Despite my hours of creative expression to bring my e-book and A Medicinal Mind to life, I started to feel heavier with each passing Sunday. For you see, every Sunday for the last 170 weeks, I had shared an email message that had evolved in compassionate complexity. Compassionate Awareness and Living Mindfully (CALM), the interdisciplinary club I helped to craft out of pure love for student well-being, had grown and flourished with each successive medical and nursing school class. As we gained momentum and members on the CALM email list, my weekly Sunday email, now entitled

A *Week of Compassion,* had expanded into a collective message of hope and encouragement for those seeking to deepen practices of contemplation and self-love. While the email continued to include the practical details of various events in the Charlottesville community, many on the email list did not live in Charlottesville or even the state of Virginia, for that matter. Despite my five years in the Charlottesville community, I had only met a mere fraction of the people signed up for our list, yet I could not help but feel in my heart that I had been collectively meeting with each soul, every Sunday, for 170 weeks, to share in communal love.

Despite the selection of new CALM leadership and the assurance that the club's ethos would be carried forward after my graduation, I sank within the massiveness of this transition and held on tightly to these sacred Sunday moments.

In Hindu and yogic philosophy, there is a beautiful moral teaching known as *aparigraha*. Described as the encouragement of nonattachment and nongrasping, the teaching of *aparigraha* pushes us to have a different relationship with the present moment, our possessions, and our surroundings. For those in temperate climates, the seasons are one of Nature's great teachers of this moral blessing, showing us that as soon as we feel comfortable— or even uncomfortable—with a particular season, a new day and new weather will eventually come and ask to be let into our "little human house."

Through my own moments of explorative meditation, I noticed a struggle, a deceptive attachment to this weekly email, to the inner tranquility and altruistic sense of love I discovered with the crafting of each message. Through continued reflection, I slowly came to accept that the loving moments I associated with the writing of the email would not disappear when I ceased to be its creator.

It was time, you see, to pass the message onward. It was time, you see, to finally step away.

While I could continue on in reflection about this moment of spiritual and contentious growth, I will simply share the words that passed through me on this joyful, final Sunday—May 21, 2017—for it is only through the words themselves that I can truly tell you from what my heart was being asked to let go.

CALM Message

On October 7th, 2012, a brave young medical student named Thomas Ball started a weekly message entitled: The Mindfulness Practice Schedule. This weekly message, sent out on Sunday evenings, was created with the intention to nurture, nourish, and inspire all in the Charlottesville community and world beyond to live a mindful and meaningful life. Containing words of gratitude and heartwarming music, the weekly message and its following slowly grew, spreading its kindness to all that wished to bask in its intention to nourish and heal. In December 2013, after the dedicated efforts of then second-year medical student Thomas Ball and first-year medical student Athreya Tata, the message had its first major transformation, becoming the weekly newsletter of the new inter-professional organization "The Yoga and Meditative Practice Club for Health Sciences Students (YMPCHSS)." Thanks to the creative minds of Athreya and then second-year nursing student and copresident of the group Jane Muir, YMPCHSS quickly found a much more poetic and embodied name: Compassionate Awareness and Living Mindfully (CALM). Under their guidance and the hand of the newsletter's new author, then first-year medical student Rob Abbott, the weekly message continued, gaining new elements such as poetry, words of reflection, and news/research articles, all with the intention of instilling the values of kindness, compassion, and all things gratitude. Now, some many years later, the original weekly message: The Mindfulness Practice Schedule has grown and evolved into something entirely unimaginable at its original conception. Continuing to be birthed every Sunday from the same place of compassionate appreciation, the intention of the weekly message, now called: A Week of Compassion, has not changed.

For those interested in doing the math behind these weekly emails, this amounts to 246 consecutive messages.

One a week for 246 straight weeks.

What was happening the last time there wasn't a weekly message?

October 6th, 2012: A Few Snapshots

1. Barack Obama was seeking re-election after a fierce debate with Mitt Romney.

2. Fighting was continuing against insurgents and terrorist groups in Iraq and Afghanistan.

3. Ryan Andresen, a 17-year-old Boy Scout from the San Francisco area, was being denied the organization's highest award of Eagle Scout because he was gay.

So after 246 weeks, and more specifically, 172 messages directed from my outbox, I simply want to thank you for your presence.

I want to thank you for opening a piece of your life to sit with these words, these ideas, and the love behind each and every one of these weekly messages.

Like Thomas and Athreya, I had no idea when I first started writing this message what it would entail, how much joy it would bring, or who would bother to even read it, and I continue to be amazed by the nourishment it brings me and so many in this community. I cannot tell you enough how appreciative I am for the spaces you hold, inspiring me to continue to write, reflect, and uncover the stories, music, and poetry that make their way into the weekly message. Saying I have looked forward to Sundays is a massive understatement. I have felt privileged and honored to share my thoughts and the work of so many other inspiring human beings just like you, each and every Sunday. And while I enjoy writing this message more than almost anything else in my life, there comes a time when one must step away, take a leave, simply take a pause. Not because of burnout, illness, disillusionment, or disgust, but because I actually LOVE IT SO MUCH.

Over the past week I have reflected on the idea of taking a sabbatical from this message, and with the encouragement of close friends and family I have decided that yes, I will take a pause. Unattached and unsure of the permanence or length of this pause, I simply step away knowing that if I desire, I can come back to this message with new eyes, new ears, and a new vision for what truly nourishes us all.

May you all continue to be nourished, to be at peace, and to forever be loved.

While this final CALM message could have served as my penultimate goodbye to my contemplative sangha and the broader UVA community as a whole, my heart yearned to let every last drop of reflection find space on a worn-out keyboard.

During my five years in Charlottesville, I had interacted with hundreds of UVA medical students as well as students from surrounding states and other countries altogether. No matter our geographic home or stage of training, medical students naturally gravitated toward one another in order to grow or, in some cases, to simply survive the incredibly demanding experience of school. From these many versions of "collective student consciousness," I had witnessed how groups and communities of students could elevate one another to achieve the seemingly impossible, but also, though primarily unconscious thought, create energies of fear, isolation, scarcity, competition, and distrust. In many ways, the collective consciousness of medical school is simply a microcosm of our larger world consciousness, with each individual either elevating or hindering our collective growth to a state of unified group consciousness whereby love, faith, the provision of all human needs, and the dissolution of human separateness can be realized.

We would likely all acknowledge that we are capable of being both "the elevater" and "the hinderer"—sometimes just mere seconds apart depending on the thoughts and stories we hold on to or express. I share this acknowledgment knowing very well that I, too, can be both an "elevater" and a "hinderer," through conscious choices of pursuing either paths of elevation or hindrance in any given moment. Having felt such deep warmth and joy on so many occasions as a result of individual and communal acts of elevating love, I wanted to assure my academic peers of just how powerful a loving, grateful community can be, while also recognizing the shadow side of our immense human potentials. While I had already shared many of these reflections and my heart with my contemplative sangha through my last email, God was now asking me to share this message and its elevating intention with my entire medical school.

And so, somewhat begrudgingly, I got on my laptop and started to type once more.

UVA Medical School Message
Dear All,

You may be tired of getting emails from me and, unfortunately, I will not be directing you to free food in this email, but I hope you'll find something more nourishing in this message than food, and I sincerely thank you for even reading this far.

I thank all of you simply for your presence. Thank you.

With just over a week to go before graduation, it is hard to imagine that just some few years ago I was spending time in the anatomy lab (the old, not so clean and nice one) identifying brain structures with my classmates. And while time does go quickly, it also doesn't. Four years is a long time, and for some like myself taking the "5-year program," it is even longer, and for others doing Ph.D. and research work it could take a decade or more. It's a long time.

Thinking months and years ahead is wonderful and having an intention and vision for yourself is incredibly powerful, but the future is not years ahead. The future is actually just the summation of the present, what we do each and every day. Want to be a kind and compassionate physician? Be kind and compassionate each and every day. Want to eat more vegetables and less processed food, eat a couple vegetables and put down the Doritos each and every day. Yes, these may seem like obvious or silly examples, but they are remarkably relevant and true.

In a more abstract sense, I like to think that we are all people in transition between states of "being," "becoming," and more "being." If we simply remain in states of transition, expansion, and growth ("becoming") or thinking about who/what we want to become (skipping the challenging "becoming" process and going straight to some new state of "being"), we completely miss the present self, the present being, the opportunity to enjoy the present moment and simply be.

Medical school is full of opportunities to "become." You are evaluated constantly as part of this challenging process of "becoming." Learning something new every day is "becoming." Studying for an exam is "becoming." Gaining more clinical insight during your clinical clerkships (at 5 a.m.) is "becoming." "Becoming" is okay; we need "becoming," but we also really need "being."

I spent most of my early life "becoming," and only "becoming," because I was good at it. If you are receiving this message now you are also very likely to be quite adept at "becoming." But it wasn't until I took time away from this "becoming," to rest and discover how to truly "be," that I could ever make peace with the "becoming" process.

What does "being" look like? For me it's engaging in creative exploration through writing, spending time in nature, meditating, practicing yoga, reading nonmedical literature, growing my Christian spiritual faith, and sharing a hot beverage with a close friend. There are tons of ways to "be," but often, these ways of "being" fall away to make room for "becoming" and only "becoming."

As many of you have probably heard me say before, I genuinely care about all of you. Even if I have never met you in person, I care about you. I want you to be happy, healthy, and free from suffering. I want you to succeed and be surrounded by joy. I know medical school is challenging, but I also know it can be incredibly rewarding.

If you are hurt, depressed, depleted, tired, burned out, exhausted, disillusioned, physically sick, broken, I am here for you. We are here for you. There are many people in this community here for you.

Four years ago I was depressed, hurt, sick, depleted, simply done. It took a long time to finally ask for help, but I did. I simply asked for help. I finally accepted it was okay to be vulnerable, to say I didn't have the answers.

I didn't start the interdisciplinary group Compassionate Awareness and Living Mindfully (CALM) because I thought it would look cool on a résumé, or because mindfulness and yoga were becoming the "in" thing. I did it because I perceived a deep need in our community to remain healthy and build resilience through "being."

I didn't care if just one person started meditating with me or if no one came to any of our events. I just wanted people to know we cared about their well-being. I understood meditation or mindfulness practice would not be some people's "thing." It's okay. We are all okay.

Over the past 4.5 years I've seen tremendous strides made in the School of Medicine to prioritize your well-being, to promote and provide you with opportunities to renew and simply "be." I've helped to grow partnerships with the School of Nursing to hold retreats, FREE retreats, and days of self-care to promote your flourishing. Once again, it's amazing to see all that can happen in 4.5 years.

But it is only the beginning, and YOU ALL are the ones to carry it forward, carrying the torches and holding the spaces for each other to learn and be nourished, to "become" and to "be." We simply cannot just keep adding to our collective stress bucket, or adding, perhaps unintentionally, to someone else's burden or bucket. We must be aware and take ownership of the energy we carry, the words we use and the spaces we hold. Make a joke about how much work you have left to do, how stressed out you are, or how poorly you will do on a test because you haven't studied enough, it's okay, it's probably funny, but take ownership of it, be willing to accept the consequences of sharing those kinds of words, carrying that type of energy, holding that type of space.

While I may be formally graduating and leaving the medical school in just over a week, my heart and soul remain in these walls and with this community. You are all amazing people with so much passion, intelligence, and drive to change the world, and I want to do all that I can to promote your flourishing.

With that intention, I want to leave you now with one final question and thought.

Do I need some help right now?

If the answer is yes, no matter how strong or weak the yes may be, please reach out. And if you think you can wait until a summer away to heal all that needs healing, I would strongly encourage you to think otherwise.

I've been there. I get it. I needed help, lots of help, and I am willing and open to talk with you if you need help, too.

No judgment. Complete acceptance.

I hope you have a wonderful week.

Rob Abbott

Behind this email was a young man waking in quiet to perform his twenty-minute yoga practice, a young man preparing a morning meal with a podcast in his ears, a young man with his funny Osprey backpack, walking every day to his medical school home, a young man dedicated not only to the acquisition of knowledge, but to the discovery of wisdom, a young man wanting nothing more than to joyfully welcome in each and every surprising human gift that entered his life.

In the words of God through Neale Donald Walsch:

"Be a gift to everyone who enters your life, and to everyone's life you enter."

Medical school had been both my breaking and my discovering, my baptism and my funeral, my death and my birth. I simply wanted to be a gift to everyone and experience the gifts they had saved for me.

Part V

Where Will You Go to Heal?

～ 51 ～

A Bodhisattva's Vow

Family Medicine Residency
Winchester, Virginia
June 2017

Depending on your source of information, medical residency can be, well, anything. From the 2000s to the 2010s, TV portrayals of medical and surgical residency training including Grey's Anatomy and Scrubs gave many in American culture at least some perception of what medical training is like for its doctors and surgeons. While it goes without saying that these portrayals are constructed dramatizations, we can't ignore the media's impact on our views of medical training, even for those of us going through it.

As I drove through the curvy Shenandoah Hills to begin my own residency training, my eyes still wet after my departure from Selene, a solitary thought filled my mind:

What's next?

Through the mentorship of my dear friend Dr. Greg Gelburd, I already possessed both precocious abilities for holistic healing and an enduring vision to manifest my own clinic as an embodiment of the love I knew all humans deserved.

What exactly did residency have to offer me?

Right before graduation, through magical serendipity itself, I met a functional nutritionist named Ryan Hall. As our friendship sped into a future of possibilities, we dreamed of our own functional medicine clinic that would blend our expertise and expansive visions for healing and wholeness. While I struggled mightily to understand how residency would help in the manifestation of our dream, I stumbled back time and time again to the same question.

What exactly did residency have to offer me?

For outsiders, the idea of practicing medicine immediately after medical school may seem rational on the surface—isn't that the reason you went to medical school in the first place? To those in health care and the medical graduates themselves, however, the idea that anyone is ready to provide any degree of safe, autonomous medical care immediately after medical school is absolutely ludicrous. In the words of another dear friend and mentor, Dr. Tommy Wood, graduating from medical school is like getting a driver's license, and everything after that, including residency training, is when you actually learn how to drive.

As I see it, residency training in the United States is the elaborate process by which a graduated medical student develops the essential skills to become a practicing clinician within a dedicated field of specialization.

Medical school acts as the expansive initial training ground, where the student is exposed to a vast array of knowledge—much of which, sadly, becomes practically irrelevant as you matriculate further into a specialty field. Specialization is not a "bad" thing, but overspecialization and the way it dissects the functionality of the human form most certainly are. Examining other countries' medical training systems could provide a comparative examination of the residency model of the United States, but for now I will simply offer my perception that our current system—including both medical school and residency—is best described as inefficient, expensive, maladapted, and personally destructive. Let me explain.

For an individual who wants to become a traditional family physician, first comes medical school, typically taking a total of four years. Following medical school, a graduated doctor will complete a three- to four-year period of family medicine residency and/or fellowship training. As I alluded to earlier, a medical student on track to become a traditional family physician—arguably the most expansive of any traditional medical professional, will be required to obtain medical knowledge and experience medical encounters during their initial school years that will become practically irrelevant during their residency training and future clinical practice. The human mind and form can only acquire and do so much.

How much longer can we convince ourselves that we should create indebted, robotic medical professionals with an expansive knowledge of certain surgical and emergency interventions despite their eventual primary role as a technician looking into the ear of a three-year-old child and telling the mother that the child's ear looks infected and may require medication? That will be

$220,000, please and thank you. And, oh by the way, that doesn't include the money you'll need to actually live on while you can't work and are paying us.

Would it surprise you if I said that for my entire first year of family medicine residency training I saw an average of three patients in the clinic per week? Three a week! If you ask any of the students I have mentored in my own clinical practice, you will understand clearly that I believe in quality and intention of clinical instruction over quantity, but in what universe does it make sense to identify a newly graduated medical student who seeks to train as a family physician and have them spend only three to four hours a week in the clinic setting seeing a total of three patients? What else do these family medicine residents need to do?

Our current medical education and residency system produces exactly what it is designed to produce. As my dear friend Ryan Munsey eloquently says, "You are perfectly designed for the results you are currently getting." It is not a surprise to me, when you look at the inefficient, maladapted, and soul-sucking medical education system—confused as it is on whether it is trying to develop generalist physicians or organ specialists—that it produces morally injured, burned out, and indebted physicians that are incapable of practicing in the way they likely envisioned as students. To expect our current medical education system to cultivate compassionate physicians with personal practices of self-care and the professional ability to provide guidance beyond one or two organ systems is like expecting our current two-party political system to create members of Congress with expansive, bipartisan views. It is technically possible, but I am not holding my breath.

As the savant Buckminster Fuller put it,

"You never change things by fighting against the existing reality. To change something, build a new model that makes the old model obsolete."

Our current society is the most chronically sick population our world has ever known. We will never stop requiring surgeons and emergency specialists to provide critical care, but we could use a lot less of the "repair when broken care" and instead replace it with the "restore and flourish care" true healing was always meant to be. I acknowledged, even as a young physician in 2017, that I would not be the one to perform a patient's surgery, stage a patient's cancer, or deliver lifesaving medication. I acknowledged that I would not be the doctor to wean them off the ventilator so they could get out of the ICU or the doctor that would do most of the things they thought doctors were supposed to do.

I was here to be a human to help my patients more deeply know themselves, in the most loving ways my divine form knew how.

I cannot tell other human beings what they need to live; I can only walk alongside them as they find their own ways of flourishing. In the same way, I do not pretend I can tell society what it needs for itself. I can simply make observations based on our current state of being and propose, based on observed suffering and challenged compassion, that we could try a different way. While the current medical education system cannot produce physicians capable of walking alongside our chronically sick population so that they can restore an enduring sense of meaning and well-being, my hopeful heart can't help but look at the immense suffering, both in our patients and our healers, and say I was not brought into this life for anything other than to create another way.

In Buddhist teaching, we find the concept of the *bodhisattva*—an individual who dedicates their life to the compassionate relief of suffering without the creation of a pathological, sacrificial consciousness. A bodhisattva breathes in from the world precisely what they need and no more, gifting the excess of energy and matter to others who are in a state of suffering. Irrespective of religious tradition, many individuals align with the values and intention of a bodhisattva and take vows as part of their commitment to this state of living. During the transmutational night of my out-of-body experience, I was asked by a divine force to undertake such vows, without the slightest clue what a bodhisattva even was.

In what I see as the "bodhisattva paradox," individuals who consciously commit to relieve the suffering of others can only begin this journey after the conscious commitment to first save themselves. In my case, I was only able to take up the bodhisattva vow when I was physically, emotionally, and spiritually unable to actually pursue the relief of suffering for anyone other than myself. When the bodhisattva acknowledges their suffering and begins to mend the fractured pieces of the heart, the desire arises to find a similar relief of suffering for all sentient beings alike.

Through each step of my medical school journey, I faced the constant reflection of my aberrant nature within the healthcare system. The egoic mind can easily attach to these reflections and create the insidious perception of what I call "betterness by differentness." But different is not better. Different is different, and better is better. To a bodhisattva, the act of being "different" actually allows the mind and heart to open to the belief that we are all fundamentally the same. Through the complete commitment to embodying the unique person we desire to be, we paradoxically move toward a greater sense of unification and shared experience.

Becoming the same by being different.

The medical education system is not designed to produce aberrancies, to produce different. To the medical education system, different is wrapped in the cloak of fear—the fear of patient harm and the fear of forced change. When the medical education system works "well," it does not produce aberrancies, yet aberrancies still show up in unexplainable ways.

What would our healthcare system be if we allowed for more aberrancies?

We have the capacity to craft healers as artists of restoring the chronically sick so that both the healers and the sick can find the divine and deep love they hold within. We have the capacity to build robust educational structures that allow for the healers themselves to explore their own divine nature and care for themselves in the ways they wish to care for their patients. We have the capacity to train our specialist physicians to become flourishing, competent, and compassionate surgeons. We have the capacity to do so much!

We simply must allow for the belief that by being compassionately and creatively different, we will see the suffering of the collective as nothing other than our own.

~ 52 ~

When Hate Came to Charlottesville

Inpatient Pediatrics
August 2017

With the weekend off from my residency duties in Winchester, I went back to Charlottesville to stay with Selene and enjoy some rare time together. In an effort to reexperience my previous Saturday morning routine, I made the short drive from Selene's apartment to Charlottesville's downtown walking mall to see some longtime friends at our local farmers market.

After I parked outside of Dr. Gelburd's clinic and began the walk toward the market, I was hit with an unwelcome wave of negativity. Something was happening, and my heart was confused, aching, and hurt. When I turned the corner at an adjoining side street, I discovered an empty parking lot. No farmers market. Not a single tent. None of the familiar faces I had come to love and know as family.

With only mere seconds of warning, I was drawn into a crowd, screaming and running for what appeared to be their lives. It was chaos.

Still somewhat removed from the disturbing commotion, I ran back to my car, with the pulsing thought that human lives were not safe in whatever this was. After what seemed like an eternity, I finally made it to my car, with my eyes now drowning, ready to close so my heart could process what was truly going on.

I fled from the disturbing images and prayed like I had never prayed before.

God, I know not what evil and hate are happening now, but may you protect all those wishing to stand for peace and drive away those confused with intentions to hurt.

I raced back home to Selene's apartment.

Before we could even begin a conversation, my eyes were pulled to her cell phone screen, and we watched a video of violence breaking out in the streets I had previously walked upon in peace for so many years.

I didn't know what to think. This was happening in Charlottesville. Our home.

I hugged Selene, holding her with every ounce of love I could pour out of my heart. The two of us, an interracial couple trained as physicians to be healers of the physical form, were now being called to be healers of a brokenness nowhere to be found in any medical textbook. Silent, just resting in each other's being, we didn't need to use words to say what was in our hearts.

What does the moment require of us right now?

Looking into each other's eyes, without hesitation we grasped hands and started to meditate and pray.

What if no one showed up? What if everyone not aligned with the protestors' views had all simply stayed home and went about their normal, joyful day? What if we even stopped to invite the protestors to a meal so we could try to understand the story behind their beliefs?

To me nonviolence is not a path of ignorance or turning a blind eye to hate or ideas of separateness, but one that seeks to strip hate and separateness of its weapons, leaving all those carrying such ideas naked and bare of their power to generate fear, create violence, or issue hurt beyond measure.

What is one way to defuse a child's temper tantrum gone off the rails? Do not engage the child. Let them yell, let them scream, let the emotion flow. But do not engage what cannot be engaged.

I have many friends who disagree with my stance of nonviolence, of nonengagement. I had friends that stood in the streets of Charlottesville as they sought to drown out words of hate and separateness. I also had many friends who did precisely as I did, holding spaces for prayer as the energy of separateness marched outside of our physical view. In the end, we needed everybody on that disastrous day. We needed every loving act of protest, prayer, and nonviolence that we could muster.

No matter their actions, every human who consciously acted to defend love stood in solidarity for the shared values of compassion, inclusion, and acceptance. Each of these humans had and still has my deep and enduring love, even if our specific actions or beliefs in the face of separateness and hate were different. It is okay to love "different." It is okay to love differently.

For love, you see, is all we really have.

53

Hope Amid Hurt

Outpatient Pediatrics
December 2017

My first six months of residency were impossibly hard. Despite a deepening well of clinical acumen and a steadfast curiosity about the things I did not yet know, I lived in a medical world that was far removed from my perceptions of human love.

Within the first few weeks' training, I felt inappropriately targeted by some of the supervising physicians for my lifestyle medicine approach. They analyzed every action I took, from the recommendation of a lower carbohydrate diet for those with blood sugar dysregulation in lieu of medication to the choice to not utilize a computer during my patient encounters. They instilled a sense that everything I did in the clinic was "wrong," when all it really was, was unexpected, courageous, and different. In my first few months of residency, I helped patients stop blood pressure medication, resolve years of chronic bloating, improve their blood sugar through dietary modification, and improve psychological well-being without the use of psychotropic medications. Healing of the purest form was happening for all to see. But residency training does not like unexpected; it does not like different.

As I got more inquisitive about why I had been immediately perceived as stubbornly different, I learned that a resident from the program who had recently graduated shared my more holistic views on health and had been perceived as obstinate and at times destructive to the intention of the traditional training. To the residency program, I was this man's identical twin, seemingly here to destroy the fabric by which family medicine residents were trained. The road was only uphill, but I could not stop. I was here to show the world another way.

In a paradoxical reversal of power for the supervising physicians, I existed as a young doctor bleeding compassion, who desired, above anything else, to connect with his patients. I was here to utilize whatever modalities available to illuminate a way forward for my patients to ultimately relieve suffering and live more joyful lives. I was not "antimedicine"—or "anti" anything for that matter—I was simply "pro-love." Pro personalized and enduring love. I made efforts to show the supervising physicians how I sought to support my patients. I wasn't looking to declare their ways "wrong" and my ways "right"; I simply sought to show them that there could indeed be a different way.

During these first six months, I worked upward of sixty to seventy hours a week and tracked essentially every moment of my life so that I was assured of meeting all necessary benchmarks for training and not "overworking" beyond daily or weekly duty hour restrictions. Some years before, residencies had adopted weekly duty hour restrictions of around eighty hours per week, taking the previously inhumane levels of required work down to something that was just slightly less inhumane.

You have it better than anyone previously in training, I heard as I stumbled around and wondered when I would find eight uninterrupted hours to eat, shower, exercise, pray, and sleep. In all honesty, my particular residency *was* one of the mildest when compared to some of the academic behemoths that sucked up the souls of young physicians like black holes. To compare my residency to another academic program, however, was simply comparing one broken-down car to another when both weren't street-worthy.

Where do you find the love to share with your patients and the world when you are barely given a moment to find it within yourself? Where do you find the love and light within your patients when you are given a mere ten or fifteen minutes to search for it within their being? Was I so radical to suggest that I needed more time and space to love and care for myself? Was I so destructive to insist on spending more time with my patients without a screen to steal away my attention? Was I so insubordinate to share that a patient did not require medication and could cure their chronic disease with food alone?

As a prisoner who got up in the night to carve a tunnel out of his cell with a mere plastic spoon, my task within the inertia of the traditional medical education system was indeed impossible, but that would not stop me from letting them see my entire being, plastic spoon and all.

As November rolled around with its unsettled sense of "normalcy," I found myself continually driven to be with Selene in every moment I was not required to be in a hospital or clinic. With two hours now separating our worlds, I routinely drove from my one-bedroom apartment in Winchester to her two-bedroom apartment in

Charlottesville. With the company of podcasts and melodies, I drove two hours one way through the dark of night or in the early hours before daybreak to find time with her where time did not actually exist. Given her own psychiatry residency, the hours we could potentially be together each week, either in person or communicating on the phone, could be counted on our own two hands. These are the things that are not talked about in medical education. This is the humanity no one is allowed to see.

During these years of training, either as a medical student or as a resident physician, your time to be a human, your time to connect with other humans—whether it be with a romantic partner, friends, or family—is so restricted that you feel these moments, these opportunities of humanness, are like drinking holy water.

This is just what training is, they say. *It is only temporary.*

But what if, as a collective society, we started to ask instead:

Do we really want our physicians and physicians in training to be so burned out, so dehumanized, so burdened by regulatory requirements, so lacking in moments to rest, to be human, to connect with their loved ones that it is essentially impossible for them to connect with their patients to find a deeper level of healing, of personalized love?

Do I really want to support a system where I will receive care and love from medical professionals that are not provided the opportunity to fully care for and love themselves?

With the desire for a space, a margin to more deeply love myself and those around me, I also wanted the same for my peers, my colleagues, and for others in all professions—for all humans alike.

Shouldn't we, with all of our technology and abundance, be able to create an intentional society whereby every exchange of services, every exchange of energy, can leave those taking part feeling nourished because it comes from a foundation that is devoid of oppression, exploitation, or fearful overwhelm?

With miles of road to ponder such questions and heart-filled desires, I simply wanted to rest with Selene, to find a way for us both to escape the confines of medical training and enter a space of greater safety, nourishment, and love. With the one-year anniversary of our relationship quickly approaching, I also wanted to fully express my deep intention to offer her my partnership and my love, in all moments, both perfect and imperfect, both bright and dark. I wanted to find the ways to always see the divine light within her, within me, even in the darkest of hours, and to construct a partnership whereby we could share in the experience of self-remembrance, healing, and unconditional love.

Immersed in the black hole of medical education, I had not worked out the details of how we would do this, I simply knew that this unpredictable and miraculous process had begun one year earlier upon embracing her divine spirit and that I wanted nothing more than to offer this invitation, this intention to her.

In efforts to quell these spiritual uprisings, the rational aspects of my being screamed out that these wishes had no basis in my current, practical reality.

You have been together for less than a year, living hours apart, immersed in medical training structures that prevent you from even being within each other's physical presence for more than a few hours a week. You have not talked about kids, about money, about where you may one day live, all the things you have been told must be explored before embarking on a journey of sacred partnership.

Flooded with a tsunami of thoughts, I felt my soul start to laugh as if I could even remember the last time I had done anything so "rational." My soul knew the road ahead, and it was not toward planet rationality.

After I put together a rudimentary plan for my sacred invitation, I asked my friend Sam, who also just so happened to be my friend Corey's husband, to create a specialized glass ring to symbolize the eternal truth, spirit, and love I sought to share with Selene. With essentially no margin in my busy life, I picked up the ring the very morning I planned to propose. Details and planning, it seemed, were quite overrated.

As I contemplated where precisely my invitation should take place, I was taken back, two years earlier, to the small town of Staunton, Virginia, where, in the moments of approaching winter, I struggled to know with whom I would share in this miraculous life journey or whether I would ever find that person at all. During my desperate pleadings with God in Staunton, I had had no idea that in a matter of months I would meet Selene and be taken into the deepest reverie of mysterious love I would ever experience in my life.

How could I adequately share with her the mystery of my walks around Staunton's unassuming streets where God encouraged me to be patient, to open my eyes to the miracle that would one day arrive?

Some time into a forty-minute drive to Staunton, through cold and icy rain, Selene expressed her confusion about this journey. I could not blame her and was remarkably surprised that she had even agreed to go at all.

"Where in the hell are we going? It is really cold and rainy out, and my back is really hurting. I just want to go home. This doesn't make any sense," she pleaded with me.

Unable to tell here why I was driving us to Staunton and ruin the surprise, I started to cry inside as I realized my planning had been remarkably poor. Selene had every right to be upset by this ridiculous trip to a place that had little to no meaning for her.

What in the hell WAS I doing?

With berating thoughts now renting space in my mind, I fought to stave off the story of my incompetence and my irrationality. Just like the young man on the third floor of the UVA Medical Center who realized his remarkably poor insight into the practical ways to find and speak with Selene, I was pushed into a state of crumbling nihilism.

What really was the point of all this spirituality, this unexplainable love? Why don't you just be practical and rational for once?!

By the time we arrived back at the apartment, time had already helped to dissipate some of the tension and misunderstanding of my ill-advised trip. Selene and

I made a quiet dinner and we played sweetly with the members of our little zoo. The red lighting from a few scattered salt lamps brought a gentling glow to our bedroom. As the hours of our one-year anniversary ticked by, I finally decided within the softening of the night to do what only that absurd fourth-year medical student did one year earlier.

Show up and love what was in front of me.

While we rested in bed, without a shred of romanticism or sentimental airs, I pulled a ring encased in a scrap of paper towel out of my jeans pocket. As I turned to Selene, amid the unremarkable simplicity of our apartment, I shared my trembling intention of partnership and deep enduring love.

"Will you be my partner in this life?"

With tears rolling down her cheeks, we were brought back in time to the moments of our first dance with Rumi, to the unexpected ecstasy of our first kiss, to the now innumerable moments of collective synchronicity, to the deep soul bond that we most assuredly shared, to the incredulous miracle that we had somehow both persevered in life this far.

Still bathed herself in the soft reddish glow of the salt lamps, and with our emotionally perceptive dog Xena nosing her way into our embrace as part of her own efforts to understand the poignancy of this unexpected moment, Selene found a voice for her soul's reply.

"Of course. You never had to ask."

⁓ 54 ⁓

Imposter Syndrome

Outpatient Family Medicine
Front Royal, Virginia
February 2018

There's a common phenomenon in essentially all professions, most prominent with medical education during early residency, known as "imposter syndrome." Imposter syndrome is best described as an internal feeling of inadequacy, of unpreparedness in young physicians soon after they begin to care for patients who see them as "their doctor." Much of the questioning young residents put themselves through as part of this complicated internal dialogue surrounds the fear that, at some point, their patients will see through the facade and find a doctor who, perhaps, cannot fully care for them in the ways they expect. Everyone can remember the first time the training wheels had to come off the bike, the trepidation felt with each cyclical revolution that could either signal a fall or a continued movement forward. The stakes of a simple fall from a bike, however, seem a much easier risk compared with a human life.

While in practical terms, the actual risks for medical mistakes within residency programs are often lower than that in nonresidency hospitals given the redundancy of care, these trends do not and cannot eliminate the mental dialogue of inadequacy and overwhelm that young residents naturally go through.

Given the tremendous support of the hospitalist teaching physicians and our associated nursing staff, I transitioned rather smoothly through the initial phase of imposter syndrome, but by early 2018, I experienced an emergence of an entirely new form of it—one of challenged faith my heart had known would one day come.

While I spent approximately 90 percent of my time outside of the family medicine clinic working in inpatient hospital settings, taking part in lectures, or performing night shift duties, I spent one afternoon a week at the family medicine clinic where I would see three to four patients of my own. Over the course of a few months in early 2018, I noticed that many of my patients had, per the front office staff's notes, actually requested me specifically. By this point, I had developed a very small online presence around my website A Medicinal Mind where I shared blogs, poetry, and podcasts with the help of my dear friends Rhett Deverich and Tucker MacDonald. I also had a listing on the Institute for Functional Medicine's (IFM) searchable practitioner directory that detailed my current clinical training and location. As no other clinicians were listed on the IFM practitioner directory within my geographic region, it appeared that those wanting a more integrative and holistic clinician were finding my directory listing and making appointments at the residency clinic. The only problem?

No one would rationally schedule a visit to see a resident.

I vividly remember my first patient, her host of chronic conditions, and her desire to utilize a combination of diet, lifestyle, and supplement therapies beyond her current medications to improve her well-being. She had worked with many other well-seasoned integrative practitioners, but had found her way somehow into the residency clinic to sit with me, a human who had barely been a doctor for eight months.

What precisely could I offer that other intelligent integrative-minded clinicians and even the traditional doctors at our clinic could not?

This was an entirely new breed of imposter syndrome, one I desperately needed to face and transmute into supportive medical guidance.

During my pause for prayer and meditative reflection before I entered each patient's room, I recited elements of a passage given to me by my friend Amy some years before. *God, may I be an open vessel to bring forth precisely what it is that this human requires in order that they may be relieved of suffering and able to live a more joyful life.* As I moved into the unique worlds of my patients, I utilized the skills I possessed as a clinician and as a human being. With the acknowledgment of my limitations alongside my accumulated gifts, I sought to be fully present with my patients within our small bubbles of healing mystery.

What else was there to do?

As my first year of residency moved further along toward its completion in June 2018, my limited schedule in the outpatient clinic filled with those who wanted to hold space with me. The patients did not care that I was a first-year resident. They did not inquire where I had gone to medical school. They were simply drawn by the pursuit of integrative medicine and a deep desire to find a clinician who could perhaps help them to unearth their inner wisdom so that they could live with more ease and joy. The universe was bringing me the individuals I was destined to help—even if it was just three people a week. I was living out my vision, my deepest purpose, unexpectedly inside the walls of a traditional medical clinic, in a town that most did not know existed, in a world that was mightily losing its way.

≈ 55 ≈

As the Wheels Came Off

Internal Medicine—Hospital
July–August 2018

Somewhat miraculously, I made it through my first year of residency. With more sleepless nights than I could count, more moments of cognitive and physical fatigue than I ever wished to endure, I completed my first year of postgraduate medical education in family medicine and was now eligible by the rules of the state of Virginia to obtain a full medical license. While a full medical license for a second-year resident is typically irrelevant, something told me I needed to climb the next rung of the professional ladder as quickly as possible. I did not have time to waste.

Each state medical board determines its own requirements for the issuance of a medical license. In the majority, a medical school graduate must complete at least one year of postgraduate residency training before they can get a full license. A smaller fraction require two years. Some still actually require three. Somewhere in this confusing and convoluted system lie logic and reason, I have no doubt.

While a full medical license is the primary requirement to practice medicine in the United States, nearly all practicing physicians also have a separate certification in some field of specialty. From family medicine and neurology to cardiology and nephrology, physicians must complete various types of residency and fellowship training followed by a comprehensive specialty-specific exam before they can finally obtain their board certification within a respective specialty. Outside of the logistical elements required to obtain this type of certification, the residency training serves as the practical arena in which a physician becomes competent within an area of specialization. This was the traditional road. But "traditional" has never been my middle name.

With the beginning of my second year of family medicine training, I was consumed with an enduring thought:

I am not actually interested in becoming a traditional family medicine physician. This is not my purpose. This is not what God intended for me.

At various times throughout my first year, I had found myself in procedural situations where I could hardly tolerate injecting a small amount of local anesthetic so that I could suture a patient's wound. I found myself deeply troubled with the initial care of newborns with all the injections, the separation from mom, and the smothering fear of bacterial overwhelm. I struggled more and more to envision a world where I could continue to perform such procedures or provide such care and find an enduring fire of meaning and joy.

If I have been called to be an integrative and functional medicine physician, why am I still in a family medicine residency?

As these thoughts percolated, I could not help but also think of Selene and her own challenges. Although we were now engaged, we were still physically removed from each other given our individual training requirements. Our fleeting moments together were grossly inadequate. While it can be rather easy to deny and suppress our own suffering, it is an entirely different endeavor to watch helplessly as a loved one suffers. The more I observed Selene's challenges, I couldn't see a way where we could both finish our respective medical trainings apart from each other.

Before I could even begin to rationally construct a plan to find my way back into proximity with Selene, to assist her in her own journey, God invited me into a new experience of the world.

For the start of my second year of residency training, I began a hospital rotation at a smaller facility in Front Royal that operated in connection with our family medicine residency clinic. As part of the rotation, I worked with a third-year resident and a supervising physician to take care of the family practice patients that required hospital care or emergency room consultations. While I had developed a decent working relationship with all of the supervising physicians in our family medicine residency, my first week on this rotation was supervised by a newly hired attending physician with whom I had experienced significant challenges and antagonism during my first year.

Within the first few days of the new hospital rotation, I discovered that the ER, which routinely paged the residents to consult on our patients, did not have my correct pager number. Instead of sending a message to me so that I could respond to a consultation request, a message would go to a former resident now living in Oregon. I only discovered the paging error after I received a curious text message from the former resident himself. While the error would eventually be fixed, the damage had already been done. The ER staff saw me as lazy and disrespectful.

To make matters worse, as part of an ER consultation where I evaluated one of our patients for potential heart issues, I was asked by the antagonistic supervising physician to prescribe a medicine that was not clinically indicated. In my opinion, not only was this medicine not clinically indicated, but I was aware of recent research that suggested its use could be harmful to patients like mine who had elevated blood sugar.

As I fumed internally at the prospect of being forced to prescribe something I did not feel was warranted, I shared my concerns with frustration and a raised voice.

Unfortunately, in the middle of the ER, with the third-year resident right alongside, this conflict of perspectives was out there for all to see. I was the lowest on the hierarchy, so to essentially everyone else who witnessed this conflict, I was grossly out of line.

Within days of this incident, I was targeted by more ER staff after another inexplicable conflict. After responding "late" to another patient consultation because of the paging issue, I was greeted by a disgruntled assistant who was not fond of my "lack of responsiveness." After I turned away from her to try and complete my task, I found the head ER physician engrossed with some activity on his cell phone. While I sought to get his attention and hear his thoughts on our mutual patient, I heard the assistant jammering away to anyone who would listen about the incompetency and laziness of residents. Stuck between disrespect and misunderstanding and distraction, I turned back to share a few thoughts with the assistant.

"I understand your frustration, ma'am, but I don't think you understand the situation entirely and I do not appreciate what you are saying about me and the residents as a whole."

As if he had been waiting for some auditory cue, the ER physician suddenly blurted out, "Do not walk away when I am speaking to you!"

Before I could even turn back to address the ER physician, a third verbal arrow came from another nurse on the other side of the small ER.

"I am going to go and speak with my supervising physician and supporting resident. I'll be back to see the patient when things have calmed down," I said into the newly erupted firestorm.

What in the hell was going on?

The next day I was asked to meet with my residency director. He shared that he was deeply disappointed in my behavior and had me sign multiple misconduct forms that acknowledged my "lack of professionalism" and "insubordinate behavior." He told me that the ER staff had even threatened to essentially ban me from the ER so that I would not be able to complete an upcoming rotation. While I was able to finish the rest of my hospital rotation, including ER consultations, and worked well with the other supervising physicians without further incident, the antagonistic supervising physician gave me a failing evaluation.

The wheels were starting to come off the wagon.

As August rolled around, life continued to spiral disastrously. During a newly developed obstetric rotation, I found myself again in the crosshairs of another antagonistic and intimidating supervising physician. Just returned from a lengthy vacation to a newly organized rotation, she was someone I hadn't encountered before. Communications weren't great, and I struggled to understand what she desired of me many times. Despite working well with the other supervising obstetricians, I was always in the wrong place and doing the wrong thing when it came to her. I felt that rather than taking a rational approach and collaboratively troubleshooting miscommunications as part of a new rotation, she jumped to reprimand me for "unprofessional behavior" and an inability to complete residency duties properly. And this was once more escalated to my residency director.

Unbeknownst to them, during this period of compounding professional humiliation, I routinely hid in our residency call room, lying on a bed in the fetal position, crying out to God asking why this was happening to me. If I weren't in the call room trying to hide from the world, bathing in my overwhelming feelings of humiliation, I was home alone, sleep-deprived, hardly willing to get out of bed. My divine light was starting to get dangerously dim.

How could I show up to work in this state and help patients? Who was here to help me?

My internal voices continued:

I am a compassionate and loving doctor. I take ownership of my choices and their potential consequences, but why is there so much antagonism, so much hurt? Does it really have to be this way?

My passion for helping others, for leading my patients through their darkest moments of suffering and into joy had been decimated in a matter of weeks. While I had never actually taken a sick day in my professional life, even as a cashier at Bass Pro Shops, I started requesting them so that I would not have to be in the hospital and feel like a humiliated shred of a human. Sickness goes by many names, and the illness I was experiencing was "a separation from love."

Despite this period of accumulating suffering, I crawled out from the depths on occasion to find hope and meaning in a new collaboration with two colleagues and their organization Autoimmune Wellness. Created to support individuals with autoimmune disease seeking to address their conditions holistically through diet and lifestyle, my friends Angie Alt and Mickey Trescott invited me to be their medical advisor and to write detailed blogs about various healthcare topics that would be relevant for their audience. In addition to these writings, we collaborated to design a clinical trial to study the effects of a nutrient-dense elimination diet called the Autoimmune Protocol (AIP) for those with an autoimmune thyroid disease known as Hashimoto's thyroiditis. Through Mickey and Angie's wizardry, we utilized a crowdfunding campaign to raise $10,000 to cover the cost of the labs I would employ in the study. To orchestrate and conduct such an endeavor as a sole independent researcher at a nonacademic institution while also working as a second-year resident was downright preposterous, but the downright preposterous was seemingly the only thing I wanted to do.

As my journey of downright preposterous with Angie and Mickey unfolded, I received another unexpected invitation from the universe in the form of an email from holistic psychiatrist and healer Dr. Kelly Brogan. In her message, Dr. Brogan invited individuals in her wider audience to volunteer in her efforts to expand clinical research into the role of lifestyle medicine to address chronic psychological suffering. After I read her email invitation, I immediately responded, without any aspect of my rational mind allowed to take part, to introduce myself and share my admiration for her work. I also informed her that I could design and carry out a randomized control trial to study the role of her online lifestyle program to treat individuals with major depression. After I hit the send button on my email to Dr. Brogan, my rational mind couldn't help but interject that I was entirely insane.

Where in the hell are you going to find time for this? And why in the hell do you think she will even read your email that will just be another slew of words in a sea of passionate messages?

Two days after my email, I received a personal reply from Dr. Brogan. She was in. She wanted me to build a study team.

With roads of meaning and joy being paved right alongside interstates of humiliation and pain, I was asked mere weeks after Dr. Brogan's reply to meet once again with my residency director in his office. Not entirely sure what the meeting was about, I entered a room with no less than four individuals including the assistant director and the chief resident. I was presented with a list of accusations, incompetencies, and incongruencies of my resident performance in a nearly twenty-page document.

You have repeatedly demonstrated unprofessional behavior and disobedience to supervising physicians. You do not utilize computers during your patient visits and are not timely with your patient encounters. You recommend treatments that are unsupported by the medical literature. You seem to be clearly working on outside activities when you should be working on residency duties, and this is unacceptable. You do not engage in any social activities with the other resident physicians or staff. Some nurses have complained that you have been in the clinic without wearing deodorant and this was distressing to them and the patients.

The list was extensive and far-reaching. No aspect of my character or actions was seemingly left untouched.

After we reviewed this document together, I was told that I would be placed on probation. As part of the probation, I would not be allowed to attend an upcoming conference to present findings from my own research during medical school. I would not be allowed to actively contribute to my personal blog or podcast. I would not be allowed to participate in the autoimmune research study that had already been approved and was set to begin in a matter of weeks. I would not be allowed to launch the new study with Dr. Brogan. My vacation days would be all but eliminated, and my prospects of spending time with Selene would be essentially erased.

As if I weren't humiliated enough, the residency director indicated that this was the first time that they had placed a resident on probation in many years and his offer was a generous one given my incompetence and unprofessional behavior.

I cried as I signed the probation document and sat to take everything in. With little time to collect my thoughts and emotions, I exited the office with reddened eyes and a wilted heart. As if things couldn't get more ridiculous, I found myself walking past the CEO of the entire hospital system, who for some reason was in our very own family medicine clinic.

As he came toward me with an open smile, he asked how I was doing.

"I'm good. Yep. Totally good."

With my afternoon clinic about to start, I had no time for more tears, no time for reflection or mourning. Patients were waiting. The downright preposterous was here in all its unmistakable forms.

56

Coming Home

Obstetrics and Emergency Medicine
August–October 2018

After the longest day of my medical career, I crashed into bed to finally explore the profoundly unthinkable. As I raced through the myriad of possible scenarios for my life as a healer, I continually returned to the ultimate question.

Do you choose residency training or do you choose your life?

It might seem melodramatic to crystallize my situation down to this existential question, but this was exactly what it felt like in the rapidly evolving maelstrom. I was being asked to essentially forgo all the elements of my life that provided me with joy and meaning.

How was this not choosing training or choosing life?

As I played through the mental gymnastics of every potential path forward, I felt immobilized with fear. I had committed over nine years of my life toward an autonomous medical practice. Throw in the four years of overachievement in high school and I was now over thirteen years into the fifteen-year journey to become a board-certified medical doctor. I was at mile marker 22 of the marathon.

Who stops at mile marker 22?

I was making no progress with my racing thoughts, so I turned to my computer to check on the status of my Virginia medical license. Despite the barriers of a technologically challenged Department of Health Professions website, I navigated my way to the provider portal. Imagine my astonishment to discover at that auspicious moment that my licensing application had just been finalized.

I was a licensed medical doctor in the state of Virginia.

Somehow, someway, as I moved through the destruction of my physical and spiritual being, and now the greatest professional humiliation I could have ever imagined, I had reached the top of the mountain. I had obtained the credential I had yearned for ever since I had been a confused college student just trying to get an A in physical chemistry.

I fucking did it.

After an exhilarating sprint out into the dark of night, I called Selene to share in the unraveling mystery.
Beginning with a rather sarcastic tone, I jumped headfirst into the earlier events of the day.

"So I met with the residency director today, and they put me on probation. As part of the probation, I won't be able to do anything outside of the residency, and they're even taking away my vacation days. It's fucking insane. Ever since June, it's been one ridiculous thing after another. I can't do this anymore. I'm going to leave."

With cautious gentleness, Selene replied, "They really don't deserve you and don't understand what you have brought to their program. The whole system is fucked. I am struggling not having you here with me. I miss you, baby."

"I miss you, too. I just don't even know if I can walk back into the clinic. I had to see patients after the probation garbage today, and it was awful. I just want to come home and grow my own practice and be with you, help you stay afloat, and give more to the animals. I can leave this residency madness. I have my license, and I know I can do it," I replied with growing confidence.

"I know, baby. I want you here, and I know you can do it, too."

After I returned to Charlottesville for a full weekend together, Selene and I assessed the immensity of the opportunity before us now. As I struggled to organize the financial and practical plans I needed to manifest in order to leave my residency, Selene continually returned our attention to my mission of why I had ever come to Earth in the first place.

"I want you here. We will do this together."

In late spring 2018, my nutritionist colleague and dear friend Ryan Hall and I had begun our lifestyle medicine clinic. While I functioned simply as an organizational and overseeing presence given my residency obligations, Ryan worked with patients to provide them with lifestyle and nutritional guidance on their journeys back to health. We had always intended to expand the clinic toward the end of my residency, but the rapidly evolving state of affairs screamed out for a markedly different timeline.

After a phone call with Ryan, we jumped headfirst into a sea of muted elation. We were going to do this *together*. We were going to do this *now*.

As the trajectory of leaving residency to pursue my own medical clinic and research interests snowballed, I reached out to some of my closest medical mentors and colleagues. Would leaving residency early be the greatest professional mistake of my life? Would leaving residency be committing professional suicide?

I met over tea with my medical school mentor Dr. Gelburd and relayed all the professional scenarios I had pondered. While he recognized that I wanted to get out of my current purgatory on probation, Dr. Gelburd was quite concerned that the resignation would limit my future professional opportunities. With his clear-eyed understanding of the professional medical landscape, Dr. Gelburd painted the best picture he could of the diverging paths staring me in the face. As we looked into the beyond together, he reiterated something we both knew in our hearts:

"If there is anyone who can take the road less traveled, it is you, Rob. It is most certainly you."

When I returned to Winchester and my clinical duties, I expressed to the residency director my desire to take a leave of absence to use the remainder of my paid leave to make some space for personal contemplation and healing. In this moment—removed from the rawness of the events that had led to my probation, removed from our numerous difficult conversations, removed from my director's challenged understanding of my healing approach, removed from the residency policies that had decimated my sense of well-being—there emerged the most improbable instance of human connection.

He said, "You have your medical license now, Rob. You can practice if you wish. You are going to be an incredible doctor, and I know you will help people in ways I can't fully understand."

My residency director wasn't a hateful or hurtful person. He wasn't there to make my life miserable for the sake of sadistic joy; he was simply an excellent craftsman within the current version of our medical education system. His factory made wheels, and he made damn good wheels. The problem for me?

I wasn't meant to be a wheel.

Across the country, we have hundreds of "wheel factories" that make good wheels, guided by factory directors who follow strict guidance from the "wheel factory overlords" on the proper way to make wheels. Amid the sea of wheel factories and the commandments from those wheel factory overlords, however, some factory directors are beginning to recognize that not only is there more than one way to make a wheel, but that perhaps, we shouldn't be making wheels at all.

While each medical training institution has its own culture and ethos, on the whole, these "wheel factories" are not the problem. The individual directors of these wheel factories are not the problem. The problem is that we as a society have yet to realize that we don't actually want wheel factories. We haven't fully realized that we don't want wheels that arrive already worn and only able to fit on one type of car. We haven't fully realized that we don't want wheels that inadvertently lead us sliding off the road.

We don't want these wheels.
We don't want this way.

As the month of September crept by and I struggled to complete my residency duties before a temporary leave, a new metaphor for my life curiously emerged. As a replacement for the myopic metaphor of the medical marathon, I suddenly saw with a crystallized vision that I, indeed, did not want the destination of a family medicine residency or any residency at all, for that matter. I did not want any of the discomfort and the suffering of the residency journey. I had driven the metaphorical hour to the airport and had even taken two legs of flights to get to LAX. Now, as I sat on the tarmac aboard my last flight, the attendant notified the cabin that this plane was going to Tokyo.

I did not want to go to Tokyo. This was not my plane.

We as a society will invariably find ourselves on planes to Tokyo, when in fact, we want to go to London. For reasons our souls do not readily understand, we stay on the plane. There is nothing wrong with going to Tokyo after all—unless you are trying to get to London.

My choice to leave residency was not quitting at mile marker 22 of the marathon, it seems: It was simply getting off the plane to Tokyo.

As the days bled into the October sun and my mornings met Selene's warmth and our dogs' jubilance, the existential epiphanies continued to crash in.

If I can be of service to fellow humans on their journeys back home to themselves, creating and holding this space on my own terms, why wouldn't I?

If I can live a life in this present moment with Selene, with my Charlottesville community, with this much joy and space for simply being, why would I choose anything else?

I did not know exactly where I hoped to go, but it was not Tokyo. It could never have been Tokyo. It was time to get off this plane.

After a silent drive back to Winchester to finalize my resignation, I went to the main hospital to collect my personal items from the resident call room. Stopping at my locker, I removed a broken stethoscope, a few textbooks, stained white coats, and a ripped pair of scrubs. Back in one of the bedrooms, I stared at the unmade bed and the off-white walls of the windowless room. As I took a deep breath for the first time in this grief-laden space, my attention filled instead with the radiant and boundless hope beckoning to me from my new future.

Tomorrow, I would wake up for the first time as an adult with no occupational or academic expectations. I would wake up for the first time with no external requirements to go anywhere or to do anything. I would wake up for the first time as a human being and not as a human doing.

I was finally coming home to embrace my loves.

I was finally coming home to heal.

Epilogue

After I returned to Charlottesville in October 2018, Ryan and I grew our integrative medicine and nutrition practice Resilient Roots. At the time of this writing, we have helped over seven hundred patients improve their health through dietary and lifestyle practices and now operate as a collaborative team that includes a health coach, patient coordinator, and additional patient assistant. In April 2019, I published the first study to demonstrate the efficacy of the nutrient-dense elimination diet known as the Autoimmune Protocol (AIP) as part of a multidisciplinary, online, and community–based health coaching intervention to improve quality of life and symptom burden in a small group of women with Hashimoto's thyroiditis. In July 2020, as part of my collaboration with Dr. Kelly Brogan and a team of supporting medical students, I published findings from a randomized controlled trial that demonstrated the numerous health benefits of a self-paced, online, lifestyle intervention for individuals with major depressive disorder.

From 2018 to 2021, I wrote medical articles for Autoimmune Wellness as part of their mission to help individuals with autoimmune disease find a more nourishing state of health through diet, lifestyle, and integrative therapies. Outside of my primary clinic in Charlottesville, I work virtually as a clinician and as the director of research for the Ruscio Institute for Functional Medicine where I collaborate with our growing team to improve the practice of integrative and functional medicine. In addition to my clinical duties, I work as a community preceptor for nurse practitioner and medical students who are looking for clinical experience in the fields of integrative and functional medicine. While I stopped posting new content for A Medicinal Mind at the end of 2019, the website still houses hours of creative exploration, and this ordinary poet has yet to stop typing on his little phone keyboard.

Chase your joy, for if you fall, you can only fall into love.

Acknowledgments

I cannot see any other way to begin sharing my grateful heart than to thank God for giving me a second chance at life, for showing me in the most illuminating of ways that I, indeed, had a deeper purpose for being alive. Without you, there would be no book at all.

From here, the list of souls to thank becomes nearly endless. I thank my parents for never questioning the ridiculousness of my unorthodox journey and for supporting me in every way possible. I thank Dr. Jacqueline Bussie for the incredible insights and support that helped this science-drenched doctor without a collegiate English class to his name find love in the editing and writing process. In addition, I am indebted to Brooke Shaffner who provided invaluable guidance to bring greater life and clarity to the manuscript and to Ashley Benning for her splendid refinement of the final manuscript. I thank the patients that have invited me into their lives in the most courageous and vulnerable ways imaginable. I thank the many souls of my "spiritual and psychological council" who have guided me as I guide my own patients to greater states of compassion and awakening. I thank my late grandfather Anthony Abbott for leaving behind his joys, his sorrows, his everything through his written works so that I could discover the miracles in this life through his curiously created road map. To the many individuals stitched into the fabric of my being who did not make it onto the page, you know who you are and I thank you immensely for your presence in my life. Lastly, I thank you Lora for being the brightest source of love and nourishment during the most unexpected of dark times and for encouraging me to never give up on this story and to never give up on love.

About the Author

Rob Abbott, M.D. is the integrative physician at Resilient Roots: Functional and Evolutionary Medicine and is a clinician researcher with the Ruscio Institute for Functional Medicine. He has authored peer-reviewed publications examining the efficacy of dietary and lifestyle therapies to treat chronic disease and is a preceptor for students who desire clinical experience in functional medicine. In his free time, Dr. Abbott enjoys trail running, poetry, and reflective practices. He currently resides in Charlottesville, Virginia.

www.ingramcontent.com/pod-product-compliance
Lightning Source LLC
Chambersburg PA
CBHW030230170426
43201CB00006B/173